The Scepter Extended

Women Warriors Ready to Rise and Shine

Endorsements

MK has done it again! Another charming page turner. Insightful! Get it as soon as you can!

Kevin Basconi, Founder and CEO, King of Glory Ministries International, Author *Angels in the Realms of Heaven*

What a powerful book that encourages women who have a call of the Lord upon their lives. The Scepter is Extended: Women Warriors Ready to Rise and Shine shows women how to walk in the power of God to defeat the enemy and see incredible breakthroughs, miracles, and healings in their lives, friends, and those they minister to.

Janie DuVall, Producer and Host of Last Days Encounters & End Time Prophecy; Creator and former Producer of Sid Roth's It's Supernatural TV

I recommend this powerful book The Scepter is Extended: Women Warriors Ready to Rise and Shine for women and women's ministries. It's also a great small group study. I thank our Heavenly Father for placing this vision in MK's heart and that she was obedient to write it for this season. It has encouraged, strengthened, and challenged my faith to be more and do more with what He has placed in my hands. Let us all answer the call to be women warriors and receive the scepter from our King of kings, Jesus.

Evette Corbin, Founder and Director of Seed Faith Ministry New York City

The Scepter Extended

WOMEN WARRIORS
READY TO RISE AND SHINE

by

MK Henderson

The Scepter is Extended

Women Warriors Ready to Rise and Shine

Copyright © 2024 by MK Henderson

Brand New Images Inc.

ISBN: 978-1-892-555-199

All rights reserved. No portion of this book may be reproduced, stored in a retrieval system, or transmitted in any form or by any means—electronic, mechanical, photocopy, recording, scanning, or other—except for brief quotations in critical reviews or articles, without the prior written permission of the publisher.

Disclaimer: This book is for informational purposes only. While every precaution has been taken in the preparation of the book, neither the author nor the publisher shall have any liability to any person or entity with respect to any loss or damage caused or alleged to be caused directly or indirectly by the information contained in this book. Most names and identifying details have been changed to protect the privacy of individuals involved.

Unless otherwise noted, Scripture quotations are taken from the New King James Version®. Copyright © 1982 by Thomas Nelson. Used by permission. All rights reserved.

Scripture quotations marked (AMPC) are taken from the Amplified Classic Edition, Copyright © 1954, 1958, 1962, 1964, 1965, 1987 by The Lockman Foundation. Used by permission. www.Lockman.org

Scripture quotations marked (KJV) are taken from The Authorized (King James) Version. Rights in the Authorized Version in the United Kingdom are vested in the Crown. Reproduced by permission of the Crown's patentee, Cambridge University Press

Scripture quotations marked (NIV) are taken from the Holy Bible, New International Version®, NIV®. Copyright © 1973, 1978, 1984, 2011 by Biblica, Inc.™ Used by permission of Zondervan. All rights reserved worldwide. www.zondervan.comThe "NIV" and "New International Version" are trademarks registered in the United States Patent and Trademark Office by Biblica, Inc.™

Scripture quotations marked (NASB) are taken from the (NASB®) New American Standard Bible®, Copyright © 1960, 1971, 1977, 1995, 2020 by The Lockman Foundation. Used by permission. All rights reserved. lockman.org"

Printed in the United States of America.

Dedication

To my loving mother,

The late **MA Henderson**,

A woman of moral character and godly wisdom who developed a warrior mentality. To this generation of women warriors, may you fulfill all that God desires for you in your destiny as we train to reign for eternity!

Ana Mendez,

Apostle, prophet, and a general in spiritual warfare from whom I learned much regarding high level warfare. Her Voice of the Light conferences and resources have been a great benefit to me in my overseas work.

Doris Wagner,

Deliverance minister and one who travels throughout the USA and overseas even when facing huge personal challenges. Her life has been a great example during my times of trials and testing.

Beverly Pegues,

A woman of excellence and director of Window International Network, coordinating prayer in the least evangelized nations of the world, the 10-40 Window.

God has not given us a spirit of fear, but of power and of love and of a sound mind (2 Tim 1:7).

OTHER BOOKS BY MK HENDERSON

Supernatural Encounters with God
The Catalyst for Healing

25 True Personal Stories of
Activating God's Healing Power
(Also available as eBook on Amazon)

Creating a Supernatural Lifestyle
Angels and Miracles

Does God use angels to bring miracles?
Find out in these true accounts of miracles.
(Also available as eBook on Amazon)

Supernatural Stories of Hope and Healing-
True Inspirational Reports from around the world

Exciting Transformations and death to life
accounts symbolically and literally
(Also available as eBook on Amazon)

Healing and Restoring Children at Risk

A manual for parents/caregivers of special needs children
(Also available as eBook on Amazon)

Sizzlers for Singles

A 52-week inspirational devotional of wisdom for singles
Also available as eBook on Amazon)

TABLE OF CONTENTS

Introduction	13
Ready To Be Healed of Trauma and Soul Wounds	25
Ready to Be Restored to Fulfill Destiny	37
Ready to Hear and Obey	49
Ready to Worship: The Key in Warfare	61
Ready to Be Adorned with Glory as High Priestess	73
Ready to Meet the Bridegroom?	87
Ready to War—Root Out Enemy, Structures, and Deception	105
Ready to Build the Kingdom in Miracles, Signs, and Wonders	111
Ready to Face the War with New Strategies	119
Ready to Redeem the Time for Harvest and Revival	131
Summary by MK Henderson	137
ADVENTURES IN GOD	147
Immobilized in His Presence by the Fire of God	149
Corporate Healing Manifested at School	149
Beauty Shop Deliverance	150
The Lame Walk and the Deaf Mute Sings	151
God Holds the Mountains in His Hands	152
Instant Healing of Heart and Lungs	153
Touching Heaven, Changing Earth	154
Hindu Priest Healed and Delivered:	155
The Church That was Built in A Day	156

Introduction

The enemy is always targeting women. God spoke these words from the beginning in the garden to the serpent.

> *"I will put enmity between you and the woman, and between your seed and her seed. (She) shall bruise your head, and you shall bruise (her) heel."* (Gen. 3:15, author's paraphrase)

Women, we will always be in a war, and we will always be in a war until Jesus returns to the earth to rule! All throughout the Bible, God used women warriors: Esther, Rahab, Deborah, Jael, Abigail, and others. Women conquered nations and saved their families in wars.

In every generation, God has continued to use courageous women such as, Amy Carmichael, Marie Woodworth Etter, Katherine Kuhlman, Aimee Simple McPherson, Ruth Heflin, Jill Austin, and many others such as Natalie Lloyd in Haiti, who risked their lives in foreign lands and/or gave their lives fighting against the powers of darkness ruling in those places.

Throughout history, women have made up a larger number of volunteers, Sunday School teachers, and church goers in general. Many prayer meetings are led by women, and most intercessors are women. Many of those assisting the needy widows and orphans and volunteering for non-profit organizations are women.

In this century, we are in transition. God desires to use women like never before during these end times. Women have been silenced and targeted by the enemy to keep them out of the battles. Women are God's secret weapon against the enemy, especially in countries that oppress women. Because women are viewed as weak, they are not seen as a threat to the anti-Christ system in many areas. That is, until God uses a woman to pray for another woman on the street and God restores a body part. Then the devil and his agents are threatened!

This is an Issachar season for women. God desires to pour out His favor on women like never before. He is establishing women in places of authority and power, in His kingdom and the kingdoms of the earth. Women, we must gain God's strategy, and lead and encourage others to fight in the battles ahead.

Esther was given favor in the palace for such a time as this.[1]

> A sceptre (or scepter in American English) is a staff or wand held in the hand by a ruling monarch as an item of royal or imperial insignia, signifying sovereign authority. Esther touched the end of it as a token of his well pleasedness in her, and acceptance of her; and that no harm should come to her for transgressing the law: acknowledging his kindness, and her thankfulness for it, as well as subjection and obedience to him.[2]

In this book, we are referring only to the scepter of King Jesus, not any counterfeit scepter of Satan used for evil.

It is time for women to do the unthinkable as Esther did, risking her life going before the king uninvited. We must be ready to do the impossible and give God the glory. Get ready to receive the warrior mentality and a new name. Leave behind those who refuse to see our new warrior identity. God is calling women to rise up and fight, even after being knocked down. We must focus on Jesus, our Bridegroom King and Commander in chief.

It took Esther twelve months to prepare, and we too must take time to be set apart, to prepare. King Jesus will prepare you for the new anointing He is giving to you. It is a promotion and commissioning for war.

God is bringing out the hidden ones not seeking recognition and fame. The Bridegroom King will bring you out of the testing place as you worship and throw away the pain and bitterness of the past. God delights in using the hidden ones, like David and Joseph, whom He trained to reign from a young age.

Remember, what the enemy meant for bad, God will surely turn for your good and His glory. The most beautiful flowers, such as cassia, grow in the most difficult places and on very high elevations.

As we are set apart, our Bridegroom King desires for us to ascend to the heavenly places and sit with Him to learn from Him and allow Him to pour out myrrh upon us; become one with Him. Myrrh is used to preserve and has a sweet odor. He wants to equip us and teach us how to use the new keys He is giving us, so we will be victorious in battle.

> *The key of the house of David I will lay on his shoulder; so he shall open, and no one shall shut; and he shall shut, and no one shall open. I will fasten him as a peg in a secure place, and he will become a glorious throne to his father's house.* (Isa. 22:22-23)

This is something we have to exercise and grow into. Jesus also referred to the keys He gave us when addressing Peter.

> *"I will give you the keys of the kingdom of heaven, and whatever you bind on earth will be bound in heaven, and whatever you loose on earth will be loosed in heaven."* (Matt. 16:19)

In this book, various women of God will point out key aspects for warring and reigning from what they have personally learned out of their experiences to win every battle and be declared the victor in Christ Jesus. Warfare is different for different people, and there are also various levels of warfare. In future chapters, I will share from my personal diary how the courts of heaven are essential in setting the boundaries and exposing and judging enemies in the war. There are levels of warfare that I was unaware of until several years ago when I experienced those levels.

Prophecy: Lana Vawser—author and Prophetess from Australia. LanaVawserministries. www.lanavawser.com

> Daughters of God are in long standing places of contending for healing, not just physical healing, but emotional, spiritual, and mental healing. In the vision, I saw women stomping their feet and the sound of a hammer coming down. It was a breaking forth of a breakthrough for justice as the sound of the gavel came down. The fire of heaven fell upon the women across the earth, the fire of His presence, and His word engulfed and purified, and suddenly, healings manifested!

I heard the rhythm of the Lord's heart being released in the Spirit for a great healing revival in which women would play key roles. Suddenly a birthing was taking place, flowing from women all across the earth; a Kathryn Kuhlman anointing, a mantle of unusual astounding signs, wonders, and miracles birthed from deep intimacy with the Lord. This happened simultaneously with the miracle of their own healings, suddenly.

I saw out of the mouths of women came golden keys. The Lord said these are keys of strategy and wisdom, and their words would carry weight to unlock. Golden leaves fell from the tree of life.

Now a huge commissioning was taking place over these women being sent, some going in prayer and others being sent physically. The keys were strategies rooted in the Word of God to bring healing to the nations. The Lord said, "I'm sending them forth in boldness, not afraid of man, but who will stand in awe of who I am.

They will be known as reformers. The fire that tried to kill them only formed them. I was with them in the fire. Now they go forth carrying the fire of My presence and see healing revival wherever I send them. They will have boldness in the revelation of who I am and bring fear upon the enemy camp because of who I am in them!"

Jesus continued to speak, "Now it's time for a scene shift of victory—they will be commissioned to lift up My name with My glory, strongly upon them, with boldness of anointing to see signs, wonders, and miracles that will draw the world to Me with a healing and evangelism anointing."

There will be stadium events where the daughters of God will minister to thousands—more than Kathryn Kuhlman, and the power of God will be displayed like never before. Yet all will be looking at only one . . . Jesus, communing with the Holy Spirit and dancing with Him. The world, media, and nations will pay attention, and it will be reported far and wide what the Lord is doing . . . all for HIS glory.

Prophecy: Lana Vawser

The battle is raging around the daughters of God. Life changing impartation is coming from My spirit NOW! Don't back down. Strike the ground! Stand up and mark your territory. Let your voice be heard in new arenas and areas. I've given you clarity, wisdom, and keys of revelation for the Word of God, also dreams and anointing to unlock the revelations of God in different spheres of influence. You will see breakthrough, and a kingdom-extended move of God. I'm raising up Esthers with strategy from heaven, and confusion and fog are being broken off.

Receive and release revelation to bring reformation. Esther, decree My Word and nations will shake and be shaped! Speak up in this season to see deliverance. No silence. Decree and it will be established.

"Yet who knows whether you have come to the kingdom for such a time as this?" (Est. 4:14)

"You will also declare a thing, and it will be established for you; so light will shine on your ways." (Job 22:28)

"Behold the days are coming," says the Lord, "When the plowman shall overtake the reaper, and the treader of grapes him who sows seed; the mountains shall drip with sweet wine, and all the hills shall flow with it." (Amos 9:13)

It will happen fast, and you won't be able to keep up. Blessings will be pouring out like wine. Past and present promises will be fulfilled.

Now, knowing your authority, speak with full conviction, faith, and boldness as My words manifest quickly. Be established as an establisher. Everywhere you walk, decree acceleration suddenly with joy. It's time for new beginnings. Life begins again!

Prophecy: Marina McLean—Prophetess

For all hidden women warriors: God will give clear direction as new doors are opening. Be cautious as God has reserved the connections for you and wisdom to know how to use them with God's specific timing. I have prepared a place of safety for all workers, birthing, and protections. You will know when to use connections and high-level favor and new doors. You are still hidden for now by My divine protection. I'm keeping your ministry out there, but you I am keeping hidden.

A few years ago, a friend and I were praying together, and she saw a vision of Jesus holding out His scepter to me. What an awesome privilege to have favor from and be invited by the King of kings, our Bridegroom King, to enter and come closer to Him! Of course, I was excited and thrilled, having no idea how my life was going to change drastically from that day on as I accepted the invitation.

It was time to rise and shine. First, God was reconfirming my new name, Esther. I was being prepared for something but was unaware as to what the preparation was leading to. Three months prior to that day, Jesus had urged me to double my prayer and worship time which was usually two to three hours daily. I obeyed and began enjoying the extra time with Him. Now I wondered why He was showing favor and extending the scepter to me. He wanted me close by His side, one in the Spirit.

Little did I know that betrayal was on the horizon, leading to a repeat of the Elijah showdown with the prophets of Baal, with me being in the role of Elijah. A David and Goliath confrontation was also in the near future, with me being in the role of David. I was living in a country where less than 2 percent of the population were believers, so these developments shouldn't have been surprising. Yet, I was taken by surprise.

Today, women are on the front lines. The Lord leads us in the fiercest battles. We must rise up and shout a victory shout. God has an undaunted place for us; we can no longer be intimidated and discouraged.

Women, we can't be pitiful and powerful for God at the same time.

God is asking, "Where are my Deborahs, Esthers, and Jaels?" They finished well. God was working for them, and He is working behind the scenes for us as well. We are not alone in the battle. He is with us, teaching our hands to war and increasing our discernment.

We walk by faith and not by sight, fully trusting in our Commander and Chief, Jesus Yeshua, the Christ. All armies have a banner, and the Lord is our banner, Jehovah *Nissi*. His banner is one of LOVE, which covers us.

When God does miracles, signs, and wonders, He is showing His extreme superiority to the devil. When this happens, I believe the demonic powers weaken over a territory. That is one of the events that happened in my adopted country when an entire neighborhood and business district saw the miracle of a woman's foot being crushed by a motorcycle and restored completely new by Jesus.

Signs and wonders like gold dust, heavenly scents, and gold fillings in teeth, all show God's love and mercy for us. However, we must not limit God to the miracles of the last season but have the faith to go into the new. God is removing the inaccurate identity of His bride. God is calling women to wholeness so they can see the chariots of the enemy overthrown.

Never forget the power of the blood of Jesus.

Jesus didn't enter the tabernacle made with human hands. He entered heaven itself.

> *How much more shall the blood of Christ, who through the eternal Spirit offered Himself without spot to God, cleanse your conscience from dead works to serve the living God?* (Heb. 9:14)

In Moses' tabernacle, the copies of the things in heaven were covered and sprinkled with the blood of animals to purify them. Jesus appeared in the presence of God for us and put His blood on the mercy seat for us. Aaron had to appear once a year and bring the blood of animals to pay for the sins of the people.

Jesus appeared only once to put away sin by sacrificing Himself. It was the appointed time for Him to do that so we could be reconciled to the Father *Yahweh*. That Jesus bore our sins is no light thing as we now have access to be with Him in the Holy of Holies, since we received Him as our Savior.

PRAYER:

Thank You, Jesus, for Your great love! I can now enter by Your blood a new and living way that You consecrated for me through the veil, as You gave Your flesh to act as my High Priest. Now I can draw near with my heart full of faith, sprinkled with Your blood, Jesus, and washed with pure water. I don't doubt and waver because You, Jesus, are faithful.

The first two chapters of this book are about being healed and restored, to prosper and be victorious in fulfilling your destiny. Women's voices are being restored. The veil of silence is beginning to be removed, as women are being healed and restored from fear, guilt, rejection, and shame. Women of God, we must be ready!

Chapter One by MK Henderson

Ready To Be Healed of Trauma and Soul Wounds

Women, we must overcome insecurities and fears to be used of God in this war. We are quick to see a task as something too difficult, too big, or too important for us to do. Therefore, we must be restored from the victimization and betrayals, etc., to be able to have confidence to prosper and go forth into what the Lord has called us to do in using our gifts.

Some of us may feel we don't have much to offer in natural abilities. We must see that our giftings and God-given abilities will enable us to prosper in whatever we put our hands to do.

We must ask God to heal our wounds so we can be restored.

We must be transparent and authentic when sharing with others to facilitate the healing in our own lives. Our hearts, minds, and souls are affected by trauma. Jesus heals all our wounds. Sorrow and grief can wound the soul as well as rejection. We must forgive those who caused wounding to our souls and give it to Jesus.

Jesus wants to take our sorrow and turn our mourning into joy. We must receive it. That is flipping the switch on the enemy. We must break out of old thought processes of doubt and unbelief and all those processes that rob us of confidence. God will remove doubt and unbelief if we ask Him so we can go into our future.

God wants to break the old cycles in our lives. He doesn't want us to be distracted like Martha, going around in circles. He wants us to progress and go forward. We can't give attention to the work of the devil, who wants us going around in circles, repeating cycles.

"But Martha was distracted with much serving, and she approached Him and said, "Lord, do You not care that my sister has left me to serve alone? Therefore tell her to help me." And Jesus answered and said to her, "Martha, Martha, you are worried and troubled about many things. But one thing is needed, and Mary has chosen that good part, which will not be taken away from her." (Luke 10:40-42)

In John, chapter 5, Jesus encounters the man lying by the pool of Bethesda. A great multitude waited for the moving of the water and the angel that came at certain seasons to trouble the water. The first one to step in was made whole of whatever disease he or she had. Jesus saw the man who had been there thirty-eight years and inquired of him.

"Do you want to be made well?" The sick man answered Him, "Sir, I have no man to put me into the pool when the water is stirred up; but while I am coming, another steps down before me." Jesus said to him, "Rise, take up your bed and walk." And immediately the man was made well, took up his bed, and walked." (John 5:6-9)

Sometimes we can be like that man, waiting for someone to come and assist us. We feel too weak to stand up on our own. The devil has lied to us, proclaiming that we can't rise up and be healed because our emotions are too damaged from the great pain and trauma we've been through. We can lose hope, just enduring our suffering.

Some of us are like the man in Capernaum, in Mark chapter 2, who was uncertain of reaching Jesus and getting His attention to be healed. It's easier to just remain in our sins and draw pity from others. We need friends like this man, who will take action because they love us too much to let us remain the way we are. This man's friends opened up the roof of the house and let down his bed before Jesus. Jesus saw their faith and said to the sick man, "Son, your sins are forgiven you" (vs.9).

The woman who encountered Jesus walking by, who had the issue of blood for twelve years, refused to remain in her condition when she saw an opportunity to be healed. She pressed through the crowd and did the unthinkable in that day. She touched Jesus. Because she had an issue of blood, she wasn't to be out in public! She was considered unclean due to her condition.

I lived in a third world country where women and teenage girls living in villages were put in sheds until their monthly cycle ended, no exceptions. They risked being beaten if they entered the house. They were considered unclean like the woman with the issue of blood.

Rather than pressing through the crowd as this woman did, some of us dwell on our pain and trauma and retell our story time and time again to gain pity from others. We might also point out to others the injustices we have suffered to gain sympathy.

One day the Lord spoke to me in a dream in which I was offered several beautiful white garments to wear, and I knew those garments belonged to me. I also saw a pair of brown pants that I was familiar with and liked; however, they no longer fit. The Lord was telling me I couldn't go back to wearing and walking in the old brown pants, as that was my past and it was taking away from the holiness and purity He desired for me to walk in. I needed to give them up and let them go so I could move forward in His holiness and purity.

Jesus is asking women the same question He asked the man at the pool of Bethesda. "Do you want to be made whole?"

We want to be like the man at the pool of Bethesda and do the new thing Jesus is asking of us. God wants us healed and restored in every area of our lives: finances, past defeats, health, and wasted years.

Trauma causes anxiety and fear to flourish, yet the benefit of it is that it can change our thought processes and cause us to think out of the box and gain fresh spiritual power. But first, we must work through the trauma and fear and move past the traumatic event.

Ask the Lord to help you move past it. Exercise your faith, as it works in love. Ask the Lord to remove all doubt so you can make confident decisions. Take a good look at your doubts. Let them work in your favor by preparing you to remove the roadblocks for the future and quickening your intuition. What is it that you are doubting and struggling with? Point it out and overcome the lie of the enemy.

Turn that trauma into a turntable on the devil by: thinking outside the box, developing meaning out of the trauma, seeing the trauma through God's eyes, and breaking out of isolation. Request others to pray for you because a better future is coming. Jesus has the final say in your life—not the devil!

The spirit of man will sustain him in sickness, but who can bear a broken spirit? When Jacob believed Joseph had been torn apart by a wild beast, he refused to be comforted.

> *He said, "Without doubt Joseph is torn to pieces." Then Jacob tore his clothes, put sackcloth on his waist, and mourned for his son many days. And all his sons and all his daughters arose to comfort him; but he refused to be comforted, and he said, "For I shall go down into the grave to my son in mourning." (Gen. 37:33-35)*

God has a healing remedy for the wounded spirit. Wounded ones must receive God's comfort. It is found in Jesus words.

> *The Spirit of the Lord [is] upon Me (the Anointed One, the Messiah), to preach the good news (the Gospel) to the poor; He has sent forth as delivered those who are oppressed [who are downtrodden, bruised, crushed and broken down by calamity]. (Luke 4:18 AMPC)*

Jesus came with deliverance and healing . . . for all. That includes healing of inner wounds. This should bring hope to those of us who are wounded and have spirit/soul hurts.

> *This hope we have as an anchor of the soul, both sure and steadfast, and which enters the Presence behind the veil, where the forerunner has entered for us, even Jesus, having become High Priest forever according to the order of Melchizedek. (Heb 6:19-20)*

Faith is the substance of things hoped for, the evidence of things not seen. (Heb 11:1)

Hopelessness is an enemy of healing. Hope is the first step to healing the wounded spirit.

Now may our Lord Jesus Christ Himself, and our God and Father, who has loved us and given us everlasting consolation and good hope by grace, comfort your hearts and establish you in every good word and work. (2 Thess. 2:16-17)

Now may the God of hope fill you with all joy and peace in believing, that you may abound in hope by the power of the Holy Spirit. (Rom. 15:13)

Paul prayed for the afflicted that they might be comforted.

The comfort that comes to the wounded spirit brings inner healing.[3]

What are the symptoms of a wounded spirit? Those who have a wounded spirit experience a hurt and ache within. The pain never heals. Although time may bring some relief, it is like a tender wound that is easily reinjured by a simple bump or scrape. Then the wound becomes fresh and painful all over again.

God is the only source of comfort and healing. One cannot receive from God without trusting him.[4]

Rachel also refused to be comforted. She was hopeless and her spirit was broken.

"A voice was heard in Ramah, lamentation and bitter weeping. Rachel weeping for her children. Refusing to

be comforted for her children, because they are no more." (Jer. 31:15)

There is hope in your future.

I know the thoughts that I think toward you, says the Lord, thoughts of peace and not of evil, to give you a future and a hope. (Jer. 29:11)

When David discovered his family had been taken at Ziglag, his soul refused to be comforted. Refusing to be comforted is a choice, according to your will.

Hope and faith must arise for us to be able to receive comfort. When one allows God's comfort, she can arise above her past. The source of comfort is God the Father, His Son Jesus, and the Holy Spirit. God promises us comfort.

"I will pray the Father, and He will give you another Helper, that He may abide with you forever. The Spirit of truth, whom the world cannot receive, because it neither sees Him nor knows Him; but you know Him, for He dwells with you and will be in you." (John 14:16-18)

How can a wounded spirit receive comfort?

One must not seek revenge against those causing the wounding. Esau wanted comfort through revenge after Jacob stole his birthright. He wanted to kill him.

So Esau hated Jacob because of the blessing which his father blessed him, and Esau said . . . "I will kill my brother Jacob." (Gen. 27:41)

One must not seek comfort through immoral behaviors and addictions. One can receive comfort by casting all concerns upon Jesus.

> *Therefore humble yourselves under the mighty hand of God, that He may exalt you in due time, casting all your care upon Him, for He cares for you.* (I Pet. 5:6-7)

One must have a forgiving heart and pray as Christ taught us to pray.

> *And forgive us our debts, as we forgive our debtors.* (Matt. 6:12)

One must have hope and faith in God.

> *The hope of the righteous will be gladness, but the expectation of the wicked will perish.* (Prov. 10:28)

God admonished Jeremiah to give up distrust and despair to receive God's comfort. When you have experienced God's comfort, you can comfort others.

> *Blessed be the God and Father of our Lord Jesus Christ, the Father of mercies and God of all comfort, who comforts us in all of our tribulation, that we may be able to comfort those who are in any trouble with the comfort with which we ourselves are comforted by God.* (2 Cor. 1:3-4)

We also partake in Christ's suffering.

> *He is despised and rejected by men, a Man of sorrows and acquainted with grief. And we hid, as it were, our faces from Him. He was despised, and we did not esteem*

> *Him. Surely He has borne our griefs and carried our sorrows.* (Isa. 53:3-4)

Remember, Jesus took upon Himself all of our sorrows so that we can be comforted

> *And about the ninth hour Jesus cried out with a loud voice, saying, "Eli, Eli . . . My God, My God, why have You forsaken Me?"* (Matt. 27:46)

Jesus was also abandoned and forsaken, and He knows that pain and sorrow of trauma is difficult to overcome. But with God's help it can be healed!

Life happens, and there were times in my life when I experienced deep wounding by those close to me. However, God healed me, and I have been able to forgive and forget. This is receiving comfort. It didn't happen suddenly, but over a period of time. I allowed the Lord to heal and comfort me. I didn't want to carry the baggage of the past with me. I wanted to be relieved of it. So, I chose to forgive and forget.

Not everyone you forgive will be able to establish a good relationship with you as some people may choose not to acknowledge their wrongdoings. You can still forgive them, but you may or may not be in relationship with them anymore. That is as long as your heart is not against them but for them and you wish the best for them.

We must also stand up to the enemy and not take his bullying. We order the enemy out of our lives every time he tries to butt in and interfere with God's plan for us.

As you keep moving forward in your healing process, God will honor that and bring healing to your body, mind, and spirit. You will notice your emotions will also heal. Remember, all the struggles we've had in our lives help to make us stronger. God never wastes our experiences, even painful ones.

As you are healed from the past like the woman at the well in Samaria, then you are able to bring godly counsel to others. Ask the Lord to give you confidence and courage to break free of your fears so you can boldly fight in His army.

One day a child was discussing butterflies with me as she was wearing them on her clothing. I commented that I also liked butterflies. She proceeded to tell me that the butterflies reminded her of how we are like them. We live in a cocoon, and we must push our way out of it so we can be fully formed into a butterfly and can fly away. She added, "That's how we grow!" Out of the mouth of babes!

PRAYER:

Dear Jesus,

Please heal my soul wounds. I give You my broken heart, Lord Jesus. Create in me a new heart and soul. I command Satan and his demons to loose my soul, specifically my mind. Angels, break and sever every negative soul tie. I command the fragmented pieces of my soul and heart to return. I take back every piece that I gave to others. Come Lord Jesus. Fill my heart with dunamis power and heal my wounds now. Bring peace and release the spirit of GOD over me and in me. Heavenly Father, Jesus and the Holy Spirit, fill my mind and soul with Your presence. May I have love and a sound mind full of grace and peace. I receive healing in my mind, will, emotions, body, and spirit. In Jesus name, I am free. Amen.

In the next chapter, my friend and mentor, Apostle Barbara Wentroble (www.barbarawentroble.com) shares her great insight regarding restoration and fulfilling your God-ordained destiny.

Chapter 2 by Barbara Wentroble

READY TO BE RESTORED TO FULFILL DESTINY

This is the acceptable year of the Lord, and He requires brokenness and humility. He is removing the dead wood and refining us for new levels of intimacy so we can walk in the new!

God is also shutting doors and forming new doors for us to go through and be established. We must shut doors to the old and transition into the new. Esther was in a time of transition in the palace. God was removing the old from her life as she was being raised by her cousin Mordecai. She was obedient to him as a father figure in her life. Esther found favor as soon as she arrived in the palace and was given maids and the best of living accommodations.[5]

Today God is also separating, choosing His bride. He is searching for those who will be obedient. He is apprehending women in profound ways to rise up like never before.

Over the years I have found myself in high level offices in anti-Christ nations with a history of abusing women. (God opened that door.) Today, Jesus is positioning women to make a difference in this earth. Twice I was in Afghanistan meeting with high level leaders, also in Indonesia speaking to 5000 believers where children were praying and prophesying!

Jesus had women as followers, and the first evangelist was a woman—the one at the well in Samaria.[6] Women were the first to witness the resurrection of Jesus at the tomb.[7] He is giving women power to bear the good news.

I had a great fear, a fear of speaking in public. My identity was that of the fearful one. God set me free and He wants to set you free.

The devil hates women, yet it's an incredible time to be alive. God is now opening doors for women in this hour. He is forming His Esther company this day. Several years ago I was speaking at a church conference and gave an altar call for apostolic women. As I laid hands upon them, the power of God came like a million volts of electricity.

My friend Naomi Dowdy had a vison of many women apprehended by the Spirit of God. He is breaking open something with women and shifting us into a new place.

Women! This is your hour as God is getting ready to do something with women that the world hasn't seen before! Women are God's secret weapon who can gain entrance into places where men don't have access . . . so go in and have tea!

There are a couple of things we need to do to be ready:

Ask God for the Issachar anointing to understand the strategic opportune times.

Ask God for favor for this opportune time. We need favor now. Esther earned favor. We pray for the favor of the Lord to be released.

Closing Old Doors and Opening New Doors

It is time for closing old doors. Esther had to change her identity from an orphan to a queen. She appeared the least likely person to be chosen as queen.

God will not leave us comfortless. He has put a dream, a vision, a calling inside of us. God will revive your forgotten dreams. Don't try to figure it out. Sometimes we get boxed in thinking about how God will do something. Don't try to box God in. Just say, "Yes, Lord." Give Him permission to order your steps.

Your life circumstances don't matter to God. When mother and father aren't there, God will take you up. If you have an orphan spirit, you can't go into the place God has for you.

In I Samuel 16 God wants Samuel to change, and He asks him, "How long will you grieve over Saul?" Don't let the grief of rejection and false accusations hold you in the old season. Close the doors and deal with the inadequacies in your life. Inadequacies leave in the presence of God.

We are quick to tell the Lord, "I can't do it!" Yes, He knows that we can't, and He gets all the glory when we do. God is faithful even when we are not. He equips and empowers us.

We don't know who we really are until we really know Him. He calls our real identity forward. We're in Him and He is in us. Reading and listening to His Word heals us, and as we obey Him, we become who God created us to be.

Only in His presence, beholding Him, we're changed into his image. What we worship is what we become. We are changed into the image of the one we worship. We must close doors to the past and focus on where He is taking us.

How do we allow new doors to form before us? First, receive a spirit like that of the apostles of Christ, that no matter what happens you can get up again. You are born for such a time as this. You will come under attack as not everyone will be excited about your call.

Second, receive your new identity. I notice that overseas, new believers change their names to biblical ones, e.g., Esther, Deborah, Aaron, Elijah, etc. Your old identity will keep you in an old place. Others may not want to come into your new identity, and some relationships are toxic. They can't be fixed. Leave it to the Lord and be around those who encourage you. Don't be around dead people, but anointed people. Close the doors to relationships that hinder you.

As he thinks in his heart, so is he.[8]

As you think so you are! You live out what you believe about yourself. Don't receive a lie from people or circumstances. Your new identity authorizes you to be in a position of authority. Esther was no longer seeing herself as an orphan, but a queen with authority.

Is rejection again knocking at your door? Don't open that door. Keep it closed. It has no power over you. Former masters of your life have no power over you.

> *They are dead; they will not live . . . You have punished and destroyed them, and made all their memory to perish.* (Isa.26:14)

They are dead, and they cannot rise up and return; even every memory of them shall perish. Tell inadequacy and fear that you refuse to give life to them.

Joshua was mentored by Moses and was a warrior, but after Moses died, Joshua became a leader of a nation. He must have a new identity of himself to lead.

> *These are the names of the men whom Moses sent to spy out the land. And Moses called Hoshea the son of Nun, Joshua.* (Num. 13:16)

His name was Hosea when he followed Moses, but now his name had become Joshua.

Hosea means "salvation." Joshua means "Jehovah is salvation." There are various teachings as to what this change means. One is that Joshua's name would remind him of who was leading the Israelite people into the Promised Land.[9]

God changes our identity at different times based on what He is going to do with us.

Close the door to every old thing that is trying to shut out your destiny in God. You can no longer say, "I can't do it". You were born for such a time as this. The Lord has come to give you a new identity.

Favor to Defeat the Enemy

New doors are forming before us. In Esther, chapter 5, it says that on the third day Esther put on her royal robes. We are now in the third day, past 2000 years since Jesus. Hebrews speaks of God removing the garments of the past and giving us new ones. Because of the shed blood of Jesus, we don't have to carry the filthy garments of the past.

Religion has you focus on the sinful past, unworthiness, guilt, and condemnation. Jesus' blood stops all of that, as He removed our sins as far as the east is from the west. We are no longer looking at who we were, but now focus on Jesus.

Esther came to a moment in time created just for her. God is raising up Esthers wearing royal robes. God is placing His crown of anointing on us at this time. This is a crown of consecration.

Esther had been in a hidden place to prepare for this time. She was hidden for twelve months.

> *Each young woman's turn came to go in to King Ahasuerus after she had completed twelve months' preparation, according to the regulations for the women, for thus were the days of their preparation apportioned: six months with oil of myrrh, and six months with perfumes and preparations for beautifying women. Thus prepared, each young woman went to the king.* (Est. 2:12-13)

Twelve is the number of government and apostolic; the spirit of sent ones to do what God has called them to do. For example, Jacob had twelve sons who became the leaders of the twelve tribes of Israel. And Jesus appointed twelve apostles to follow Him.

There are many now who are smelling like the anointing, and some are in the hidden place, not on TBN or Charisma magazine, but soaking in God's anointing. He is about to bring them through the door, with the aroma of the High Priest, the aroma of God.

God has an Esther company approaching the door today, smelling of the Lord. These women are hidden and prepared for destiny, like David in the cave of Abdullum. Some of you feel like you are in a cave and people don't care what's going on in your life.

The Holy Spirit is like Mordecai pacing back and forth checking on you as he checked on Esther. This is not a permanent place but a place of preparation. During difficult times my husband used to say, "It came to pass." That means it didn't come to stay!

David was alone, forsaken and abandoned, but it was not permanent. David had already been anointed. Some say life is a bowl of cherries, but someone came along, ate our cherries and broke the bowl.

We hear pilots say, "We are in a holding pattern." Sometimes we feel like that, suspended in space. David was in that place, and it seemed as if nothing was happening, not going anywhere. However, it was a place of testing. This place was a Masada or a Masuda. A Masada is a testing place to become better. A Masuda is a place of temptation to become bitter. We choose what kind of place it will be for us. Will we become better in this place, or will we become bitter?

I give the devil no credit for anything! God has won every victory in every holding place. We must say, "I'm going to forgive and not become bitter. I will come out in the power and anointing the Holy Spirit."

This was the attitude of Joseph in the prison pit, wrongly accused with the lies of Potipher's wife. God didn't forget Joseph, and He has not forgotten you. He knows exactly where you are, and you will come out fully prepared. Genesis 50:20 tells us Joseph told his brothers that what they meant for evil, God meant for good.

No matter what came to keep you from your destiny, God will take care of everything that has happened and use it for your good. You will begin to see the dawning of a new day. The Esther company is positioning herself to come out.

David's men of war, rejected, discouraged and depressed with a religious system that had nothing to offer them, held on to God. Like David and his men of war, when in that hidden place we learn to hold on to God as there is nothing else to hold onto. When you are in the hidden place you discover your true friends.

This is a time of preparation like David fighting the bear and the lion. These seemed like big enemies at the time but prepared him for Goliath. And the cities and territories he conquered later. You, too, can be prepared to be a victorious warrior.

The Esther company is coming into a higher place in God.

> *Behold, a door standing open in heaven. And the first voice which I heard was like a trumpet speaking with me, saying, "Come up here, and I will show you things which must take place after this."* (Rev.4:1)

In the verse above, John was in the spirit realm, not the earthly realm. The apostolic sees potential in you as you carry an anointing to unlock that which is inside of you.

It's time for us to put our heads in the clouds and come up and look around heaven to hear the Father, Son, and Holy Spirit. Stand before the Lord in His presence. That is the privilege of the new covenant. We can come up and hear what God is saying.

> *But we all, with unveiled face, beholding as in a mirror the glory of the Lord, are being transformed into the same image from glory to glory, just as by the Spirit of the Lord.* (2 Cor. 3:18)

We are changed as we behold Him, and we're becoming who we were created to be. We ascend positionally.

> *He worked in Christ when he raised Him from the dead and seated Him at His right hand in the heavenly places far above all principality and power and might and dominion, and every name that is named, not only in this age but also in that which is to come.* (Eph 1:20-21)

> *But God, who is rich in mercy, because of His great love with which he loved us, even when we were dead in trespasses, made us alive together with Christ (by grace you have been saved), and raised us up together, and made us sit together in the heavenly places in Christ Jesus.* (Eph 2:4-6)

We also ascend progressively when in communion with Jesus, becoming one with Him. We sit with Jesus in intimacy

The new open doors lead to restoration and governing authority.

> *These things says He who is holy, He who is true, "He who has the key of David, He who opens and no one shuts, and shuts and no one opens. I know your works. See, I have set before you an open door, and no one can shut it; for you have a little strength, have kept My word, and have not denied My name."* (Rev. 3:7)

We now have authorization and the key of David, prophetic eyes and ears to know and understand the purposes and plans of God that's on His heart.[10]

> *Because you have kept My command to persevere, I also will keep you from the hour of trial which shall come upon the whole world, to test those who dwell on the earth. Behold, I am coming quickly! Hold fast what you have, that no one may take your crown. He who overcomes, I will make him a pillar in the temple of My God, and he shall go out no more.* (Rev. 3:10-12)

Women, arise and fulfill God's call! God is seeking and calling for the Esther Company now. What has already been bound in heaven we can bind on earth. You are now authorized to do it. Things tied up in heaven must be tied up on earth.

> *"Assuredly, I say to you, whatever you bind on earth will be bound in heaven, and whatever you loose on earth will be loosed in heaven."* (Matt. 18:18)

The Esther Company is coming forth wearing the crown of anointing, and royal robes, extending a scepter of authority with the key of David. The Esther Company arising in this hour is clothed with glory and authority. Now receive the key of David with governing authority on this earth.

The king asked Esther, "What is your request?"

Specifically, what do you want?" The King of kings is now asking us the same question. He has promised to give us the nations. Esther's assignment from God was to save a people group. What is your assignment?

Women, the cassia anointing of God is for us. Cassia is one of the herbs in the anointing oil for the High Priests, growing at high elevations. We must go through the door and receive the anointing to go up higher, being lifted up in victory!

PRAYER:

Dear Lord Jesus,

I am ready to be restored to fulfill destiny. Please show me, Lord, what I need to do to be restored completely. If I need to take time to pull aside and rest from my labors, help me to do just that, regardless of what others may think or do. If I need to wait upon You for my restoration, help me to wait so that I can mount up like an eagle when the time comes for me to fly like an eagle.

You are restoring me, Lord, and giving me a solid foundation so I can stand strong under pressure.

> *We have this treasure in earthen vessels, that the excellence of the power may be of God and not of us. We are hard pressed on every side, yet not crushed; we are perplexed, but not in despair; persecuted, but not forsaken; struck down, but not destroyed—always carrying about in the body the dying of the Lord Jesus, that the life of Jesus also may be manifested in our body.* (2 Cor.4:7-10)

> *But God has chosen the foolish things of the world to put to shame the wise, and God has chosen the weak things of the world to put to shame the things which are mighty; and the base things of the world and the things which are despised God has chosen, and the things which are not, to bring to nothing the things that are,*

that no flesh should glory in His presence. (1 Co. 1:27-29)

Lord Jesus, we depend upon You and Your love to fulfill our destiny. Not only do I wait for restoration but for Your redirection in my life.

We know that all things work together for good to those who love God, to those who are called according to His purpose. (Rom.8:28)

Chapter 3 by MK Henderson

READY TO HEAR AND OBEY

There is neither Jew nor Greek, there is neither slave nor free, there is neither male nor female; for you are all one in Christ Jesus. (Gal. 3:28)

Paul is saying men and women are equal and can hold any role by the power of the Holy Spirit. We are all made in the image of God. Yes, there are roles typically held by men such as pastor, revivalist, and evangelist; however, women have also held these positions and roles.

We must be ready to hear and obey when called by Jesus. He is our Bridegroom King who goes with us everywhere we go. Every part of the body of Christ has a function, and we strengthen each other. Unfortunately, there are still biases in the body of Christ today. We must rethink our view of ourselves as only helpmates, appendages to the men in ministry. What happens, then, if we are single and God calls us to go? Some women have married to be in ministry as they knew they wouldn't be accepted because they were single.

We should be looking for all kinds of opportunities to display God's love everywhere we go and to everyone that we encounter. We don't always need words to do that. Sometimes just being kind and thoughtful is enough. Let the Lord direct us and give us insight into the lives of others. He may also give us prophetic words to speak in any given situation for others.

We must be prepared to obey Him immediately when the Holy Spirit directs us. We must be intentional to do this. It takes discipline. We lay aside our agenda for His agenda, our schedule for His schedule. We don't expect an immediate reward in return. Sometimes the Lord speaks in tiny details and other times He paints a broad picture of what He desires for us to do. We must not negate the tiny details as unimportant and soon forget about them but remind ourselves that everything He tells us to do is important.

One day, in my adopted country, I was walking home through a business district where most of the people knew me and knew I was a foreigner. I had good relations with most everyone in that area. My attention was drawn to a beggar who was asking for money. The Holy Spirit nudged me to give the coins I had in my pocket. We don't usually see beggars on the street, and as I reached out to give the coins, I received the shock of my life. This beggar was a young woman. In all my years living in this country I had never seen a young woman begging on the streets.

As I looked into her eyes, I realized she had serious needs. Her hair had been chopped off which is unusual in this country. Women rarely cut their hair. It's a cultural taboo. As she reached out to take the coins, I realized she was reaching for more than coins. She grabbed my hand and cried, "Help me, sister!"

I could see she was filthy dirty from head to toe and her foot was wrapped in blood-stained gauze, covered with flies. She had a walking stick. I realized she was also starving, and my heart melted. Several women gathered around us to ensure I didn't try to talk to her about Jesus. In this Hindu/Buddhist country, a new law had just been passed prohibiting proselytizing on the street. I left and went home to return with my first aid kit to clean her injured foot, treat and bandage it.

Upon my return two men appeared, both claiming to be her husband. I suspect she was married to the disabled one as the other one appeared to be using them both. While I cleaned her foot, she requested I pray for her. I explained that I only pray in the name of Jesus. She said, "That is okay. Please, please pray for me."

I helped her to a nearby butcher shop where there was plenty of water and she bathed and washed. I bought her clean clothes from a nearby shop and she looked like new person. I also gave her food. The people in the area informed me that she and the men lived off alcohol and were considered hopeless.

Again, she requested that I pray to Jesus for her. I prayed for her injured foot as hostile people gathered around. One suggested I take her to the local hospital to have the foot amputated. I informed the crowd that she requested I pray in Jesus' name, and then I prayed out loud for Jesus to heal her foot. She decided to embrace Jesus right then and there.

A couple of weeks later I saw her again, totally clean, and her foot was completely restored and made new for the glory of God!

We can't be so focused on our plans and activities that we don't stop for the one. We can't be so limited by time that we miss God and what He is doing or feel that we don't have time for others because of our own responsibilities. God will manipulate time for us. He did it in a great way for Joshua, making the sun and moon stand still. He is still doing things like this for His children today.

God doesn't ask us to help everyone we see, but He directs us to those we're to be in contact with to show His power and glory! The young woman I reached out to died a few months later.

Ecclesiastes tells us there is a time for everything, so there is also a time of resting in the Lord. We must take time for replenishing our spirit, soul, and body. That means we must take time to be with the Lord in prayer, worship, and meditation. When we don't redeem the time fellowshipping with the Lord, we have nothing to give out to others.

When we hear His voice, He gives us a vision that we carry within our hearts from the heart of God. That vison may not be a common vision for women; however, if it is of God, it will come to pass.

Many visions in the Bible were birthed out of divine revelations. God prepares us first many times, then the vision comes as to what His will is for us and how He may desire to work in and through our lives. He desires to use our talents and abilities fully, although the timing of His utilizing them may not be in our timing.

In some cases, He may require us to put our talents and abilities on the back burner and wait upon Him to bring about their utilization. Remember, He is the only wise God and He knows the best time to use those abilities, skills, and passions for His glory, not for our showcase.

Sometimes we have a passion for an issue that God has placed in our hearts. He may just want us to spend time in prayer about it rather than to immediately do something about the issue. Other times He may give us divine appointments to exercise our muscles in this passion and even partner with others to see the vision birthed.

First and foremost, we must acknowledge God has given us the desires and talents and skills, etc. for His glory, and to bring souls into the kingdom. God may even lead you to do things that are completely out of the box for you, and others will tell you that you can't do that because it's not for a woman to do.

We must be ready to move and take action step-by-step to see the vision unfold as God would have it and see victory and success. Always remember that there are many times when we are stuck in past losses or victories and can't go to the next event or task to fulfill the vision. It's easier to stay in our comfort zone, rather than to step out in uncharted waters no matter how well prepared or unprepared we may be for the task ahead.

We must focus on Jesus and not the naysayers around us. We need to receive godly counsel from more mature women in the faith. Deborah and Jael did actions that were totally out of line for women and yet they succeeded. They trusted God because they knew He was with them. This is one of my favorite stories of mighty women of God in the Bible. It is recorded in Judges chapter 4.

> *Jabin, King of Canaan, had harshly oppressed Israel for twenty years, and they cried out to God, for he had nine hundred chariots.*
>
> *"Now Deborah, a prophetess, the wife of Lapidoth, was judging Israel at that time. And she would sit under the palm tree of Deborah between Ramah and Bethel in the*

mountains of Ephraim. And the children of Israel came up to her for judgement. Then she sent and called for Barak the son of Abinoam from Kedesh in Naphtali and said to him, "Has not the Lord God of Israel commanded, 'Go and deploy troops at Mt. Tabor, take with you ten thousand men of the sons of Naphtali and the sons of Zebulun and against you I will deploy Sisera the commander of Jabin's army with his chariots and his multitude at the river Kishon and I will deliver him into your hand'?"

And Barak said to her, "If you will go with me then I will go; but if you will not go with me, I will not go!"

So she said, "I will surely go with you; nevertheless there will be no glory for you in the journey you are taking, for the Lord will sell Sisera into the hand of a woman. Then Deborah arose and went with Barak to Kedesh.

Heber had separated himself from the other Kenites and pitched his tent beside Kedesh. And they reported to Sisera that Barak had gone up to Mt. Tabor. So Sisera gathered together all of his chariots and all the people who were with him to the River Kishon.

Then Deborah said to Barak, "Up! For this is the day in which the Lord has delivered Sisera into your hand. Has not the Lord gone out before you?" So Barak went down from Mt. Tabor with ten thousand men following him. And the Lord routed Sisera and all his chariots and all his army with the edge of the sword before Barak;

and Sisera alighted from his chariot and fled away on foot.

But Barak pursued the chariots and the army . . . and all the army of Sisera fell by the edge of the sword. Not a man was left.

However, Sisera had fled away on foot to the tent of Jael . . . because there was peace between King Jabin and the house of Heber. And Jael went out to meet Sisera, and said to him, "Turn aside, my Lord, turn aside to me and do not fear."

And when he had turned aside with her into the tent, she covered him with a blanket. Then he said to her, "Please give me a little water to drink, for I am thirsty."

So she opened a jug of milk, gave him a drink, and covered him.

And he said to her, "Stand at the door of the tent, and if any man comes and inquires of you, and says, 'Is there any man here?' You shall say, 'No.'"

Then Jael . . . took a tent peg and took a hammer in her hand and went softly to him and drove the peg into his temple and it went down into the ground; for he was fast asleep and weary. So he died. Then as Barak pursued Sisera, Jael came out to meet him, and said to him, "Come, I will show you the man whom you seek. And when he went into her tent, there lay Sisera, dead with the peg in his temple.

> *On that day God subdued King Jabin before Israel and the hand of Israel grew stronger and stronger against King Jabin until they had destroyed him.* (Judg. 4:3-24, author's paraphrase)

The more battles we fight, the stronger we become until we destroy our enemy.

Jael didn't disqualify herself because she was a stay-at-home housewife. Her hiddenness was to her advantage and her quick wit her weapon! The hidden ones are important to God as they deal the enemy a sudden unexpected death blow like Jael did to the captain of the enemy army.

Like Jael and Deborah, you may be called to do something great for God that no other person has done. Only you can do it! It may be an assignment from God that is unique to you and your sphere of influence. None other can do it how God wants it done. Only you.

Jesus reminded the disciples:

> *For everyone to whom much is given, from him much will be required.* (Luke 12:48)

To whom much is given, much is required. God's purpose for your life stands. God has planned out our days.

> *"Remember the former things of old, for I am God and there is no other; I am God and there is none like Me. Declaring the end from the beginning."* (Isa. 46:9-10)

Remember, He works from the end to the beginning. Victory is already there, established for us even before we begin.

If you have been given a big vision, don't doubt the outcome. Just take steps to obey God. He knows you can't do it in your strength, but you can in His strength and for His glory!

> *"Not by might nor by power, but by My Spirit," says the Lord of hosts.* (Zech 4:6)

You are a woman of destiny and called to greatness in Christ. So how does one begin? We begin as Paul said,

> *"I do not count myself to have apprehended; but one thing I do, forgetting those things which are behind and reaching forward to those things which are ahead, I press toward the goal for the prize of the upward call of God in Christ Jesus."* (Phil.3:13)

It takes faith. Abraham was a great example of a man of faith.

> *Who, contrary to hope, in hope believed, so that he became the father of many nations, according to what was spoken, "So shall your descendants be." And not being weak in faith, he did not consider his own body, already dead (since he was about a hundred years old), and the deadness of Sarah's womb. He did not waver at the promise of God through unbelief, but was strengthened in faith, giving glory to God.* (Rom.4:18-20)

> *"The just shall live by faith."* (Rom. 1:17)

We begin with a step of faith. When I was fourteen years old, I knew God had put in my heart to travel to Mexico. I lived in a small rural community of only about 600 people, and it seemed very few people there lived above the poverty level.

Yet, I believed one day God would make it possible for me to answer that call upon my life. At the time I didn't realize the call was for the nations!

At nineteen years of age, I turned down a marriage proposal because I wanted God's will to be done in my life. Soon the opportunity came for me to travel to Mexico with a friend who had a mission there. She invited me to her home to assist in helping conduct child evangelism outreaches for children in rural Mexico. I ended up traveling to twenty some countries over the years.

Recently I heard the Lord speak to me to travel to a small, mostly unknown island in the South Pacific. I did not know anyone there, but I answered that I would go when the opportunity came. Sometimes the Lord tells us to do things that do not seem possible with human reasoning. Others may doubt that the Lord is speaking to us.

It is important to listen with our spirit to the Holy Spirit for confirmation of what the Lord is speaking to us and receive prayer from a mentor if you can, once you feel that God has confirmed the assignment. Usually, when I travel to a new place there are friends with me or waiting at my destination for me to arrive. In this case, neither scenario existed. I had to totally rely upon the Lord to take care of all the details. I tried to make connections on my own, but those I contacted did not seem to be focused on the Lord's will but personal benefits of my trip. I tried to make hotel reservations, but that did not work out either. I decided that if this was God's will, I must wait for Him to put together all the details and make the connections.

When I let go and let God, everything quickly fell into place. I had connections and lodging. God also planned the itinerary for me, and I ended up speaking eight times and saw God's hand move mightily everywhere I went. Before I went, God had told me I would visit three islands. It happened just the way He planned it for me. He also told me I would meet one country leader and prepared me with a few words to give, and although I did not set an appointment, God brought us together. He told me I was to speak at a certain church, but I had been unable to reach the pastors prior to my trip. However, a couple of days after my arrival, I visited the church and was given the mic and asked to speak, without having even met the pastors.

We walk by faith and not by sight! That means we go forward without foresight, knowledge, understanding, and human reasoning. God is good and takes care of the details when we just trust Him. We must surrounded ourselves with people who have faith. God's ways are higher than our ways and His thoughts higher than our thoughts.

PRAYER:

Lord Jesus,

I know that I have a destiny because You have a purpose for everyone's life.[11] I know You have a great future and a hope for me. Help me to accomplish the things You desire for me to accomplish as life is short and I want to fulfill my destiny on this earth and do and be everything You created me for. I desire to walk by faith in hearing Your voice and I desire to obey You. Help me to hear and obey. Help me to tune out the words of the naysayers speaking negativity, doubt, and unbelief, and focus on Your power. Nothing is impossible for You!

In the next chapter, Marina McLean, worship leader, shares fresh insights on worship and warfare and the presence of God. (www.drmarinamclean.com)

Chapter 4 by Marina McLean

READY TO WORSHIP: THE KEY IN WARFARE

I have an acronym for worship that I would love to share with you. It will provide a foundation to help you understand why there is always warfare to get into the presence of God and why it is important to keep an active awareness of worship and intimacy in your life.

W-Word, you need to have a love for the Word of God because it is the foundation for knowing Him and building a relationship that is reflected in your prayer life. It will also lead you to discovering your purpose and ministry. The Word is one of the ways God speaks to you, and you will discern good from evil because you have His word as your final authority. You don't negotiate with God's Word; you obey it.

O- Open ear, the Word trains you to listen to God's Word as you read it. You hear God speaking to you and become sensitive to His voice. You learn His still voice that is quietly leading you. You won't be moved by false teaching and false doctrine, as you have been trained to hear His voice. This also happens through your prayer life, and it is seen visibly in your worship, both public and private.

R- Relationship, your relationship with God is so important. Like children know their father's voice from the time they enter this world out of their mother's womb, a child of God knows the voice of their Abba Father.

S- Spontaneity, the best worship comes from your spontaneous response in worship. There is always a level in the worship service when you stop singing the written songs that are on the screen and you add your voice print, or expression to the Lord. You begin this level of expression in your private time. You stop singing the songs you remember and the songs that are your favorites and you sing your own revelation of Him. It might be 'hallelujah,' 'amen,' or 'I love You, Lord.'

H- Heart, we are told to worship God 'with our whole heart and all our strength'. We are to engage our full expression from a heart that is pure and intimate with God. We will not be ashamed or reserved to show Him our full affection.

I- Intimacy, "into me see" is a lovely way that I love to explain intimacy. It is the act of being vulnerable and open in your nakedness before God. You are not ashamed because of your sin, pain, difficult situations, or condemnation. You are fully cognizant that you are in His Presence, and while in His presence you are healed, loved, and made whole.

P- Prayer, the foundation of your relationship that enables you to worship freely. I like to explain that when you don't know how to pray; pray the Word, and that will increase the length and depth of your worship. Your prayer life is the external witness to others of how much of the Word is within you.

Praise affirms the work of God that is presently happening. You will know Him as the God of the now. You can recall the things that God did historically for the children of Israel. However, you are bearing witness of the God who is doing miracles and giving you a breakthrough in your life. You have a personal testimony of His goodness and delivering power in your life.

Praise Him in the heights.

> *Let the high praises of God be in their mouth, and a two-edged sword in their hand.* (Ps. 149:6)

Worship brings a divine exchange. When you give God worship, it is the beginning of a response from the earth to heaven, and God inhales your worship like a fragrance. You smell something wonderful like perfumeries or good marinated food, and you start that process of inhaling the aroma. God does the same with your worship. He inhales your fragrance of worship, and He exhales His glory. The wonderment of worship continues to be intoxicating! It is a response that becomes infectious in an environment of believers, experiencing the same level of worship and response.

Worship that changes the atmosphere will bring revelation and breakthrough. Revelation is knowledge that God reveals to you while you are in His presence. It might happen during prayer, a worship service, or being still after you have done both. Your worship has provoked God to reveal His secrets to you. That is revelation. God reveals Himself in the heights. When you pour out your worship to God like the woman who opened her box of perfume and washed Jesus' feet with her tears and dried it with her hair, He will not turn us away.

> *And, behold, a woman in the city, which was a sinner, when she knew that Jesus sat at meat in the Pharisee's house, brought an alabaster box of ointment.* (Luke 7:37 KJV)

That unique expression of worship showed us that we can bring our unique expression. He will affirm us and give us a peace that will acknowledge that we are in His presence."

Praise is used as a tool to plough as it will break up the atmosphere that is full of unbelief and doubt. When there is no faith in the environment, the songs that you sing should declare the power of God, the works of God, and the meanings of His name. For example, *Elohim*—God Almighty, *Elyon*—God Most High, *El Shaddai*—The All Sufficient One. These are just a few of God's names that you should use to break up the atmosphere, to make your praise more effective, and to see a breakthrough environment.

Worship exalts the names of God. As you sing His name in a worship environment, your attention has shifted from praising Him for His works in your life to singing about your personal revelation of Him. You are now worshipping His name because of your testimony of Him as the Redeemer of your soul. Worship shows God that you know Him like a husband knows his wife. Your worship is based on the loving knowledge that you have of Him.

The Warfare

> *Then was Jesus led up of the Spirit into the wilderness to be tempted of the devil. And when he had fasted forty days and forty nights, he was afterward an hungered.* (Matt. 4:1-2 KJV)

The King James Version of the verse above gives you the visual and mental condition of what Jesus was going through. It was a moment of humanity that we can all relate to. The devil always tempts us in the weakest times of our lives. In the frailty of the situation, he highlights the emotions that will weaken our confidence, and then we second guess ourselves. Doubt and fear will definitely be the result, as weakness overtakes our faith.

> *And when the tempter came to him, he said, If thou be the Son of God, command that these stones be made bread. But he answered and said, It is written, Man shall not live by bread alone, but by every word that proceeded out of the mouth of God."* (Matt. 4:3-4 KJV)

Why does Satan highlight our condition and then make it a temptation to gain victory over us? He highlights our needs to persuade us to become dependent on him with his subtly or blatant presentation of giving us power. However, we must realize that Satan can only meet our temporal needs. He is not the source of continual freedom to our worship.

> *And they came to a place which was named Gethsemane: and he saith to his disciples, Sit ye here, while I shall pray. And he taketh with him Peter and James and John, and began to be sore amazed, and to be very heavy; and saith unto them, My soul is exceeding sorrowful unto death: tarry ye here, and watch. And he went forward a little, and fell on the ground, and prayed that, if it were possible, the hour might pass from him. And he said, Abba, Father, all things are possible unto thee; take away this cup from me: nevertheless not what I will, but what thou wilt."* (Mark 14:32-36 KJV)

Gethsemane is not a burden you can pray away; it's the place you must go through. The meaning of Gethsemane is the place of pressing, like the process of crushing grapes to make wine. It's the process of yielding to the Father and becoming totally reliant on Him for your strength and identity. Through warfare you learn who can handle your pressure and be a constant encourager. Even in His silence, you can feel His uplifting spirit.

Your heart corresponds to what you hear, and you respond like a trained ear. This is a phrase I love to express as a faith building tool to keep you edified. We can all quote "faith comes by hearing." So, what are you feeding your spirit? You must listen to faith teaching that will affirm you and challenge you to trust God. You must write Scriptures and post them in your environment so that the Word is before your eyes. Place notes on your bathroom mirror, fridge door, in your wallet, on your phone, the visor in your car, etc.[12]

Sound Dimension

Consider that the original worship sound was not from instruments but was from voices.

Could it be that the sound inside of us that comes from all the pain, all the things that we've gone through, is the very sound God is looking for—that expression of us?

"And God said, Let us make man in our image, after our likeness" (Gen. 1:26 KJV). He breathed into man and deposited His breath inside him He gave man the ability to worship God the way God always wanted to be worshipped.

What is the sound dimension when it comes to worship?

> *And God said, Let there be light: and there was light. And God saw the light, that it was good: and God divided the light from the darkness.* (Gen. 1:3-4 KJV)

God moves in the sound dimension. We clearly see that things were created and came into existence through the voiceprint of God. God creates through sound. He spoke to man through the sound dimension, and man responded and communicated back to God through his own sound dimension. Sound plays an important role in creating an atmosphere in which God moves and manifests Himself.

God shadows Himself when the atmosphere is conducive for his glory. The very meaning of the word image is "shadow." Jesus gave us the beautiful picture of this.

> *Then answered Jesus and said unto them, Verily, verily, I say unto you, the Son can do nothing of himself, but what he seeth the Father do; for what things soever he doeth, these also doeth the Son likewise.* (John 5:19 KJV)

I want to challenge your thinking with this statement: God moves in a sound dimension. The Bible tells us

> *And God said, Let us make man in our image, after our likeness: and let them have dominion over the fish of the sea, and over the fowl of the air, and over the cattle, and over every creeping thing that creepeth upon the earth.* (Gen. 1:26 KJV)

Here are God's instruction to us to sing.

> *Speaking to yourselves in psalms and hymns and spiritual songs, singing and making melody in your heart to the Lord.* (Eph. 5:19 KJV)

There is always a highpoint in worship when the worshipper is singing in the Spirit. The sound of corporate response in the atmosphere brings a heightened awareness that everything that wants to exalt itself against God is subdued and brought into obedience. The majesty of God's presence has total control and God is totally in control. All He requires of us is to be discerning and sensitive to the leading and administration of His presence.

The presence of God is tangible when you worship Him and acknowledge the fullness of His power. The display of His presence is an affirmation that He has responded to you as you create the atmosphere of worship. Miracles happen in this environment. When you create this atmosphere and are willing to administrate from God speaking to your spirit, you will begin to call out miracles and deliverance, and people will receive and testify of what God has done in their bodies.

When you have experienced warfare, you are awakened to the consciousness of God's power and deliverance in your life. The warfare, the intensity and duration, and/or how you surrendered to God is never forgotten. Your faith is built. You understand that although the enemy is fighting you now, you have the power of recall and experience to know that God will deliver you again!

> *When Jacob awoke from his sleep, he thought, "Surely the Lord is in this place, and I was not aware of it." He was afraid and said, "How awesome is this place! This is none other than the house of God; this is the gate of heaven."* (Gen. 28:16-17 NIV)

Jacob woke up in the residue of the presence from the dream, and he was still responding from the presence. The atmosphere is progressive, so you must court and keep building the atmosphere, as it's still active and working. We sing songs to confirm what God is doing in and through us.

We must come to the reality that this is a lifestyle of experiencing the presence of God in our private environment and prayer times.

Even your attitude must be conducive to His presence—your attitude attracts God, so He draws you into the intimate place of worship and revelation with Him. His presence awakens the fear of the Lord; not the fear that makes you run from Him in despair and judgment. No, it's the fear that makes you want the comfort and healing of His presence. Presence awakens your worship and sensitivity to His presence—the real expression God wants is coming forth.

> *Make a joyful noise unto the Lord, all ye lands. Serve the Lord with gladness: come before his presence with singing. Know ye that the Lord he is God: it is he that hath made us, and not we ourselves; we are his people, and the sheep of his pasture. Enter into his gates with thanksgiving, and into his courts with praise: be thankful unto him, and bless his name. For the Lord is good; his mercy is everlasting; and his truth endureth to all generations."* (Ps. 100:1-5 KJV)

> *I will sing of mercy and judgment: unto thee, O Lord, will I sing. I will behave myself wisely in a perfect way. O when wilt thou come unto me? I will walk within my house with a perfect heart. I will set no wicked thing before mine eyes: I hate the work of them that turn aside; it shall not cleave to me.* (Ps. 101:1-3 KJV)

It's illegal to come before God without thanksgiving. The Hebrew meaning of thanksgiving is giving praise to God ahead of what you receive and being in expectation of His Goodness being on display in your life.

Thanksgiving lets you enter His gates. When you practice this discipline, you will be able to sing to the Lord, even when you are being judged by Him and being convicted through the Holy Spirit to confess your sins, faults, weakness, and guilt. God can handle all your short comings and still see you as righteous when you are in His presence. Standing in abandonment of your sin and being fully immersed in the presence of God makes you perfect in His sight.

Testimony of Warfare in Worship

I lead worship in different denominations, cultures, and languages. I know how to measure the atmosphere of a church or auditorium and be ready to change the order of the set song list to spontaneity because of the absence of faith or lack of reverence to the presence of God. I also change it when I discern that we need to go higher, and I switch again from the set song list to spontaneous adoration of the Glory of God.

I will sing the songs that emphasize the blood of Jesus, victory in the resurrection power, and songs that testify of the names of God. This automatically changes the atmosphere and leads people into an acknowledgment of God's power and a sense of what the presence of God is present to administrate.

I was leading worship in an Asian congregation, and they were expecting miracles that night because the theme of the conference was the Glory of God. While I was leading spontaneous worship, a deaf woman began to hear. She testified after the ministering of the Word and the miracle prayer was prayed her miracle came during the worship. She forgot about her condition and just worshipped God. Her focus was entirely on Him.

We saw many people healed, and they gave testimony of how God healed them from blindness in their eyes and deafness in their ears. Many crippled people walked and a child with lung disease was completely healed. We couldn't count or take all the testimonies that night, but this lady's testimony stood out for me.

Worship lets you abandon your fear and anxiety when your focus is about who you worship, the living God *Elyon*, meaning the Lord Most High.

I met a lady recently that knew me from Ruth Ward Heflin's glory meetings in Ashland, VA. We were reconnecting after not seeing each other for twenty-three years. She told me I changed her life through the prophetic word I gave her and the depth of my worship. Twenty-three years later, she experienced that depth of worship in a church in Maryland, with our spiritual children Apostle Joshua and Ify Nathan of Glory Center Family Church again. As I led a spontaneous time of worship, she was led to tell me the impact and impartation of our first encounter.

The supernatural realm was opened up again and she could testify of the new realms and visions that she experienced again. She later told me that she has a deeper walk with the Lord. She changed from being a faithless believer to being full of faith and understanding the supernatural.

PRAYER:

I am reminded of the song, "Forget about ourselves, concentrate on Him and worship Him!" A song that we can make our daily prayer!

Chapter 5 by MK Henderson

READY TO BE ADORNED WITH GLORY AS HIGH PRIESTESS

The Shekinah Glory of God is very much needed in our lives today. It is evidence that God is with you as your face shines with the glory of God. Mary Magdalene, Mary of Bethany, Jesus' mother and the Samaritan woman at the well all must have had the glory of God upon them as people responded to them quickly and turned to Jesus.

I recall one of the days I was adorned with the glory of God but was unaware of it. I escorted a dozen blind and partially blind people to an eye hospital in my adopted country for cataract surgeries. This people group spoke a dialect that was not widely known, but we had a recording of the gospel message that we carried with us on the trip. For most of them it was their first time hearing this message. At the eye hospital, people began following me everywhere. I didn't realize until later when I reviewed photos taken while there that my face shone with the glory of God. In a country where only one and a half percent of the people believed in Jesus, I was honored to have an audience who inquired of me about Jesus, including medical staff.

How does one gain the glory of God? First, we must be humble. Real humility—not a fake humility. It is a position that we have, humility or pride. A humble woman of God doesn't hesitate to bow low in service to God and other people. As many things related to God begin in our hearts, so does humility as it is a mental state of our view of ourselves. Do we see ourselves as high and lifted up or do we see ourselves as Jesus saw Himself, a servant?

Sometimes events happen that contribute to pushing us into humility vs pride. In my adopted country many foreigners leave all the dirty work to the nationals, not wanting to get their hands dirty. I never understood that, as we are equals in Jesus' sight.

We rebuilt an earthquake-destroyed building and converted it into a home for girls in danger of being trafficked and sold into sex slavery. Most of the work had been completed except a much-needed balcony. For safety and security reasons it was necessary. After much searching, we located a young man to build it. When he finished, I spent a day painting it. The locals were surprised to see me painting and brought their friends to watch. Just because I was the director of the project didn't mean that I only give instructions and orders. I must also join in the work.

We are all brothers and sisters I explained to them that Jesus expects us to work together. He said the greatest among the disciples must be the servant of all.

> *"Do not be called 'Rabbi'; for One is your Teacher, the Christ, and you are all brethren. Do not call anyone on earth your father; for One is your Father, He who is in heaven. And do not be called teachers; for One is your Teacher, the Christ. But he who is greatest among you shall be your servant. And whoever exalts himself will be humbled, and he who humbles himself will be exalted."* (Matt. 23:8-12)

I wore the clothing of the culture, but I was always aware that Jesus arrays us in His holy glory garments.[13] We must live holy, pure lives and do great exploits as in the book of Daniel. As women of war, we cannot afford to compromise or have mixtures and try to serve God and mammon. We cannot serve two masters, as we will love one and hate the other. How can you fight on the side of one army and sleep with the enemy on the other side? We can't give in to critical spirits and gossip or fellowship with the wolves in sheep clothing who came from the enemy camp, having sold their souls to Satan. Instead, we can try to win them to our side.

We must recall the words of wisdom of our Godly mothers and grandmothers. The time will come when we too must pass the baton to our daughters and their generation. Prepare them well as their battles will most surely be greater than ours!

I learned from my aunt who was in a tough inner-city ministry in South Central Los Angeles yet remained humble and loving in spite of all the hardships she faced. I only wish I had spent much more time learning from her before she went to be with Jesus. I spoke with her by telephone the day she departed, and she asked me, "Are you ready to take my mantle?" At the time I didn't really understand the full meaning of the question. Today it's much different. Due to my warfare experiences, I now have a better understanding of the question.

I believe that Mary the mother of Jesus was adorned with the glory of God and so was Elizabeth the mother of John the Baptist. I don't know about you, but I desire to be adorned with the glory of God. That glory is our helper and protection!

A Royal Priesthood

A couple of years ago I was sharing at a meeting in New York with a group of believers about the signs, wonders, and miracles I witnessed God perform in my adopted country, and one of the leaders stated that God was giving me an anointing of Melchizedek. He was a high priest. I wondered what that meant for me and began researching the position.

I read about Melchizedek and about Jesus being a High Priest after the order of Melchizedek. I discovered the royal priesthood isn't just about a position or identification but also about power and dominion. The priesthood is about royalty and shares a throne with the King of kings who has all things under His feet in heaven and earth.

The life role of a king or priest is to exercise his throne room rights, affirming and confirming his authority over the devil who is trying to possess his possessions!

> *The Lord said to my Lord, "Sit at my right hand, till I make Your enemies Your footstool." The Lord shall send the rod of Your strength out of Zion. Rule in the midst of Your enemies!* (Ps. 110:1-2)

As kings and priests, it isn't important what role we play on a day-to-day basis, whether as a housewife, secretary, wife, mother, minister, or teacher, etc., but to be fully aware of God's purpose for our lives and the position where He has seated us.

I realized that one with an anointing of Melchizedek was to exercise authority and to be confident that He who began a good work in me will perform it until Jesus returns.

> *"You are a priest forever, according to the order of Melchizedek." The Lord is at Your right hand; He shall execute kings in the day of His wrath., He shall judge among the nations."* (Ps. 110:4-5)

This anointing produces results as I'm now seated with Him in heavenly places, sharing His power! The people of God shall be strong and do exploits!

> *Those who do wickedly against the covenant he shall corrupt by flatteries; but the people who know their God shall be strong, and carry out great exploits.* (Dan. 11:32)

Yes! Let that sink into your spirit right now. Meditate on it for a few minutes. Jesus said we will do greater works because He is going to the Father.

In the past few years, the Lord has been using me as a sign and a wonder to those in darkness. Paul was also admonished by the Lord, and informed that he would open eyes.

> *"I now send you, to open their eyes, in order to turn them from darkness to light and from the power of Satan to God."* (Acts 26:18)

As I was being attacked by anti-Christ people, the Lord reminded me of His admonishment to Paul. The gospel has to go to those in darkness not in word only but in power. Those in darkness must see the power of God. We have a harvest to reap now.

One night Jesus came to me and told me what He was going to do. The anti- Christ people were shocked and fearful as

He shined his light into their darkness, exposing their dirty works. They came running out of their dark place screaming.

The Lord spoke to me that I was His watchman on the wall as I trained intercessors. We could not hold our peace or keep silent but had to make mention of His name, even in countries with laws forbidding one to say His name in public. In spite of that, we exercise our faith and proclaim His name as we are joined to Jesus and we exalt His name! Paul prayed for wisdom and revelation.

> *The God of our Lord Jesus Christ, the Father of glory, may give you the spirit of wisdom and revelation in the knowledge of him: the eyes of your understanding bring enlightened; that you may know what is the hope of his calling, and what the riches of the glory of his inheritance in the saints, and what is the exceeding greatness of his power to us-ward who believe, according to the working of his mighty power, which he wrought in Christ when he raised him from the dead, and set him at his own right hand in the heavenly places, far above all principality, and power, and might, and dominion, and every name that is named, not only in this world, but also in that which is to come: and he put all things under his feet, and gave him to be head over all things to the church, which is his body, the fullness of him that filleth all in all. (Eph 1:17-23 KJV)*

We have ascended with Him who sits on the throne at the right hand of power which He worked in Christ when He raised Him from the dead and seated Him at His right hand in the heavenly places, not only in this age but in the age to come. Paul desired for the Ephesus church to have wisdom and revelation. We have the Holy Spirit to work in us and empower us to exercise this authority. It's not authority within ourselves but our faith in Jesus Christ. We speak the word of faith, boldly declaring things that be not as though they are!

We must see ourselves as being on the other side of the battle, on the victory side. Joshua saw the walls of Jericho already down when he told the Israelites, "Shout, for the Lord has given us the city!" Jesus spoke regarding the five loaves of bread and saw 5000 as they multiplied. See it and begin to declare it now and begin thanking Him for it!

> *Seeing then that we have a great High Priest who has passed through the heavens, Jesus the Son of God, let us hold fast our confession. For we do not have a High Priest who cannot sympathize with our weaknesses, but was in all points tempted as we are, yet without sin. Let us therefore come boldly to the throne of grace, that we may obtain mercy and find grace to help in time of need.* (Heb. 4:14-16)

We too can enter the heavenly realms and seek authority, revelation, and power from God's throne as we enter His presence. We desire to be transformed so that we have Christ's nature and see people and circumstances through His eyes.

When we grow in Christ-likeness, we will re-create Christ in our sphere of influence, and like Christ, we become a priest forever after the order of Melchizedek. Jesus brought the new everlasting priesthood. If the Levitical priesthood was perfect, there wouldn't have been a need for a new priesthood.[14]

He didn't come according to the law of a fleshly commandment but according to the power of an endless life. He testifies, "You are a priest forever according to the order of Melchizedek" (Heb 7:17).

> *The Lord has sworn and will not relent, 'You are a priest forever according to the order of Melchizedek', by so much more Jesus has become a surety of a better covenant. Also, there were many priests, because they were prevented by death from continuing. But He, because He continues forever, has an unchangeable priesthood. He is also able to save to the uttermost those who come to God through Him, since He always lives to make intercession for them. For such a High Priest was fitting for us, who is holy, harmless, undefiled, separate from sinners, and has become higher than the heavens . . . He did once for all when He offered up Himself.* (Heb. 7:21-27)

Jesus Christ does not need to offer daily sacrifices for the sins of the people.

> *We have such a High Priest, who is seated at the right hand of the throne of the Majesty in the heavens.* (Heb. 8:1)

> *This is the covenant that I will make with the house of Israel after those days, says the Lord: I will put My laws in their mind and write them on their hearts; and I will be their God, and they shall be my people.* (Heb. 8:10)

Because His law is written on our hearts and minds, we are in covenant with Him, our High Priest, who is also our Mediator. If we confess our sins, He is faithful to forgive us.

And has made us kings and priests to His God and Father, to Him be glory and dominion forever and ever. (Rev 1:6)

And hast made us unto our God kings and priests: and we shall reign on the earth. (Rev. 5:10 KJV)

This is not just for later, but is also for the here and now!

We have the ability to recognize aspects from the spiritual realm. As the Lord allows and gives us grace, we will actually demonstrate the ability to pass through the heavens, stepping through the temporal or earthly realm and entering into the spiritual realm.[15]

I believe Jesus saw things that were going to happen before they happened, such as raising Lazarus from the dead. Look what he said to Lazarus' sister: "He will rise again!" I believe He had already seen Lazarus rising from the dead in the spirit.

We can experience the same things as we step into the Spirit of God through prayer, praise, and worship. Here we seek revelation, authority, and power from God's throne. The mantle of Melchizedek is operating in the Spirit of God, walking in the anointing of the Holy Spirit twenty-four seven! As we become mature in the things of the Spirit, we can become a priest after the order of Melchizedek and speak what we see and hear as God directs us.

We must walk in holiness, so our spirit is free to ascend to the spiritual realms. Kevin Basconi talks about his visit to the throne room.

> I went into the throne room of God. The glory of God was everywhere. I thought, this is not good because I

know I have sin and I might not make it back out of here. The closer to the throne, the more intense the glory became. I watched as hundreds of people came and stood at the throne of God; they came and stood at the judgement seat of God. Jesus came and stood by many of them as their Advocate. Others stood alone with no advocate. When I saw the lost standing at the judgement seat alone, it made me very sad and greatly troubled my spirit. If you have the blood of Jesus covering you, He is your Advocate. It is a fearful thing to fall into the hands of the living God. (Heb 10:31)[16]

God will use women in these last days as mature daughters to see a great harvest of souls. He wants us to come into completion in Him. Melchizedek means King of Righteousness.[17] Our righteousness is nothing but filthy rags, but we can walk in the righteous of Jesus Christ by the power of His blood. Melchizedek is only mentioned in the Bible seven times and that means completions.

The high priest handles sacrifices at an altar. In the Old Testament, it was a stone altar in which animals were sacrificed unto God. Today because of Jesus Christ, it is an altar of praise and worship as we glorify the Lord God. He responds today as He did in the Old Testament with fire. Holy fire comes upon our altars as we praise and worship the Lord.

As we praise and worship the Lord, the spirit of Elijah comes and restores us, heals us, and destroys witchcraft being sent our way. We are building a superior altar of the Lord that destroys all evil altars.

What is an altar? It is a place that is consecrated to something or someone. It is a consecrated place. We meet the Holy Spirit at our altar of praise and worship. Humans exchange energy at evil altars all over the world out of ignorance. Jesus was sacrificed on Calvary as the sacrificed lamb of God on the altar (cross). We have the fire of God upon our altar of worship as the Holy Spirit manifests. God's fire can't be touched by the humans that serve the demonic.

How did Elijah kill 450 Baal prophets? One man, Elijah, controlled them as God manifested His fire power. Elijah activated and rebuilt the old altar that Israel had neglected. When the Israelites sacrificed on the altar at a certain time of day, God always came and answered them by fire. So it was not a new great miracle that God sent fire upon Elijah's altar that day. It was common for God to respond by fire when Israel was sacrificing and serving God.

Elijah had a superior altar that made the Baal altar powerless. We must get past the flesh to the altar of God and worship Him in spirit and truth. Our spirit must touch heaven as we worship. It's not just singing some songs as a ritual but touching heaven and changing the earth!

God is making us high priests after the order of Melchizedek so we can have power and authority over the enemy all the time and in everything! That is the reason we must be prepared to see miracles, signs, and wonders on a regular basis, everyday!

We keep moving forward by faith until God manifests His power through us. The throne room is a place of authority and royalty, but also a place of worship. The garments of the kingdom culture are holiness, praise and worship. We wear the garment of holiness in word and deed. This takes discipline, and it's the power of the Holy Spirit by which we are able to wear the garment of the glory of God as His high priestess!

PRAYER:

Lord, we realize we can't do anything without Your power! As high priests and kings, we surrender to Your will every day, and we come before You with thanksgiving, praise, and worship. Lord, teach us how to walk in our authority as a high priest and king so that we may do great exploits in and through You for Your glory.

In this next chapter you will see how God uses dreams to direct us and inform us of the future.[18]

Because Jesus came to destroy the works of Satan we can also declare and decree it! "And the God of peace will crush Satan under your feet shortly."[19]

The Lord will demolish and destroy the work of our enemies. We can flow in the updraft his spirit is creating.[20]

God Himself establishes the work of our hands.[21] We dwell in the secret place of His presence, covered by His wings.[22] He leads the way and brings us into alignment with our destiny and greater purpose.[23] God desires for us to rise up in faith and victory.

God's directed changes will enable us to take a turn for the better, leaving past troubles behind. He will begin to put all the pieces of our lives together so we can see the big picture from His perspective.[24] Many Bible heroes failed in some way, but God memorializes them, emphasizing their successes!

One may fall seven times and yet rise up![25] Often there is a big gap between where we are now and God's destiny for us. God gives us dreams to instill hope in us and help bridge that gap. Seeing ourselves in a new light helps erase the false identities we have received. Our choices today determine our direction for tomorrow. The choices we make tomorrow determine our future. The path of the just is as a shining light.[26]

Sometimes God repeats our night dreams until we embrace the truth and move on. Truth is critical. The enemy plants lies in our minds. We must recognize them as such. When we see ourselves through the eyes of Jesus and experience His love, fear is eradicated.[27] The things Jesus reveals to us in our dreams are eternal.[28] Therefore we look past our present circumstances seeing the eternal, birthing faith and hope.

In this next chapter, my friend Iris Nazreen reveals how dreams changed her life and how Jesus is still speaking to us through dreams to help prepare us for spiritual warfare. (www.gods-messenger.webs.com. thelordsvoicecriestothecity@gmail.com. Twitter/irisnasreen)

Chapter 6 by Iris Nasreen

READY TO MEET THE BRIDEGROOM?

- Ready to Wake Up?
- Ready to Go?
- Ready to Accomplish?
- Ready to Receive?
- Ready to Act for Redemption?

As we wear the bridal garments, we must also be ready, awake, and filled up with the Holy Spirit!

A Servant's Journey

I am a servant of God chosen by Him to warn about the signs of the End Times. My testimony is, in reality, every servant's journey. God gave me hidden manna of revelation that will help you walk with the Lord and arrive at the finish line of your calling.

> *His lord said to him, "Well done, good and faithful servant; you were faithful over a few things, I will make you ruler over many things. Enter into the joy of your Lord."* (Matt. 25:21)

I was born and raised in Pakistan. My upbringing was in a middle-class Christian home where my spiritual guide was my mother. As the head of the home, we looked to my father as a pillar of support and guidance. I am the middle child between two older sisters and two younger brothers. My family has always been a blessing from above in my life.

My spiritual connection with the Lord was always in my soul, even when I did not understand it. In my junior years I would look toward heaven and say, many times, "I love you, God." When I look back on my past, I can recall that nothing materialistic would impress me—like big houses, expensive cars, rich attire, gold, diamonds, or an impressive lifestyle. I would always wonder why people were chasing those things. Later, at maturity, I recognized that they were the "normal" majority; I was a different person. I feel like I am not of this world, as the things of God entice me.

Surprisingly, God revealed His purposes for me in a dream. The dream wasn't solely for me, but a journey for all the servants of God who are chosen and called to serve Him. This is a "Servant's Voyage" that demonstrates the repercussions of both faithful and unfaithful servants on a majestic royal ship sailing above the black ocean. The King and Ruler of that ship is *Yeshua*, the Lord Jesus Christ. In the year 1997, God blessed me with an incredible dream that revealed my purpose on earth. Please join me to explore God's plan for my life as it was displayed in this dream.

God's plan, embedded in this revelation, is the same for all His servants. In the first part of my dream, I saw black water—black as the darkest night—rushing against a grand, beautifully crafted aristocratic golden ship embedded with gold carvings. In the center of this majestic ship is the Royal Chamber, where the Lord Jesus Christ is seated on a golden royal seat. There are two cliques of people aboard this ship. One group of people is standing inside a royal chamber in the presence of the Lord. The other group left His presence and is standing outside. They are lined up around the railing of the deck of the ship, awaiting their sentence. At the bow end of the ship, two soldiers in royal garments are prepared to throw these people out of the ship into the sea. They are about to be engulfed in the black water of death and desolation.

In the second part of this dream, I found myself standing in the midst of sparkling spring water before two saints who stood in white robes. The Lord's messengers told me to go and join the laborers, who were busy repairing the house of the Lord. This house of the Lord looked like a huge temple on top of a mountain. I saw the laborers' carrying vessels filled with soil from the bottom to the top of the mountain to refurbish the ruins of this magnificent building. Their labor was filled with excruciatingly hard work that required extreme physical and emotional suffering. They carried bowls of soil on their heads and their robes were dirty with soil.

My dream of the year 1997 relates an important revelation for every servant whom God chooses for His divine plan and purpose on earth. This revelation is about three stances that God wants His servants to abide in.

Live as a Living Sacrifice for God:

God's anointed servants become living sacrifices for His service to help save souls on earth. In my dream, I was blessed to be standing before the Holy Presence of the Lord Jesus Christ and to be among His servants, who are called to serve Him and be a living sacrifice for Him. The wicked of the world and the principalities and powers of darkness kill, torment, and martyr servants of the Lord. The Lord Jesus

Christ suffered for His obedience to His Father. His servants follow the exact footsteps of their Master. They are found faithful unto death for His name's sake.

Required Purification and Holiness to Serve:

The relationship with the Lord and abiding in His Word 'the Bible', transforms us from physical beings into spiritual beings for His servanthood. The Lord Jesus Christ washed the feet of His disciples and commissioned them to preach the good news of salvation. In Romans 10:15, we read, "And how shall they preach unless they are sent? As it is written: 'How beautiful are the feet of those who preach the gospel of peace, who bring glad tidings of good things!'" Truly, I am blessed with the gift of washing my feet similarly for the purpose that the Lord Jesus Christ has called me to serve.

Build the Temple of the LORD God:

The third characteristic is the most vital responsibility that the Lord bestows on His servants. I was told by God's messengers to join His servants already working on the repair of His Temple. The temple that the Lord showed me was standing on its magnificent pillars right at the top of the mountain, but it was in complete ruins. The Scriptures provide us with an understanding of God's house. In Isaiah 2, we read a similar message about God's house established on top of the mountain.

> *Now it shall come to pass in the latter days that the mountain of the Lord's house shall be established on the top of the mountains, and shall be exalted above the hills; and all nations shall flow to it. Many people shall come and say, "Come, and let us go up to the mountain of the Lord, to the house of the God of Jacob; He will*

> *teach us His ways, and we shall walk in His paths." For out of Zion shall go forth the law, and the word of the Lord from Jerusalem.* (Isa. 2:2-3)

Wonderfully, I was handed the job of repairing the ruins of the temple after being anointed in the presence of the Lord Jesus Christ seated on His throne. I saw the temple in ruins, which indicates that humanity is shallow due to the lack of an intimate relationship with their Lord. This bruised generation is suffering for the lack of knowledge of God. They have forgotten that their bodies are supposed to be the 'Temple of God' where His presence must supersede everything else.

> *Do you not know that you are the temple of God and that the Spirit of God dwells in you?* (1 Cor. 3:16)

I can only praise the Lord God for choosing an insignificant person like me for such a mighty purpose as declaring His will to all the nations of the world. God's servants are sent to help repair the restless hearts and broken lives all over the globe.

Now, with this knowledge, you can understand the essence of the final part of my dream, in which God called me to be His servant and join laborers who are already at work in repairing the Temple of God on the top of the mountain. Therefore, all of God's servants are working in uniform for the harvest of souls. Multitudes will be saved globally and conserve their eternity in the Kingdom of God.

The restoration of God's Temple coincides with the salvation of humanity, which the Lord created with an everlasting love. Servants of the Lord are hauling the spiritual burden to heal mankind from sickness, diseases, and demonic oppression. No one can do this difficult job of releasing victims from the trap of Satan without JESUS, who is the rock of salvation. The Lord Jesus Christ has taught His servants well how to crush the head of the serpent under their heels.

Become A New Creation in Christ

After receiving the position of a servant of God, the Lord began a phase of preparation, sanctification, and transformation into a new handiwork in Him with His knowledge, love, and wisdom of the heart. I can still remember how the Lord took me over in 1997 and converted me unknowingly to become a new creation in Christ. How it happened, I don't know. But I do know that this is the most pleasant experience that anyone can ever have. Now, because of my intimate relationship with the Lord, I feel light as a feather, void of the burden of sin, independent from the slavery of the flesh—like a cloud, carefree like a dove in the Lord's holiness, and powerful like a lion in His power and strength. I could never imagine gaining it all on my own. It is the Lord Jesus Christ's grace that took me in my weakness and blessed me in His love to be His child and servant. I really cannot thank God enough.

Along with transforming me from a physical being into a spiritual being, the Lord also kept me growing in sacred gifts and equipped me with spiritual weapons to accomplish the given job. This job is filled with excruciating hardships, like laborers who are carrying a container filled with soil over their heads from the bottom to the top of the mountain to repair His Temple. God's servants are working in the exact manner that I saw in my dream. His servants are carrying the burden of suffering humanity in the power and strength of the Lord. They are equipped with the spiritual weapons from the source of all good things, the mountain and rock of salvation, whose name is *Yeshua*, the Lord Jesus Christ.

In conclusion, I would only say that after my personal experience in a loving relationship with my Creator, I feel honored to be of use to help, comfort, and edify those seeking the truth. Since 2007, God has consistently revealed prophecies for mankind in my dreams and visions. Each of those prophecies came to pass, which helped to build my faith. This trust has motivated me to serve in this mission to help humanity come to God and find refuge in His arms. It is my prayer from the depths of my heart that my sufferings and sacrifices done for the work of the Lord shall not be in vain, but that all those who will read this testimony will humble themselves before the King of the universe in the spirit of repentance and find salvation in His Name.

Prophetic Message of GOD

God has definite plans for specific times and seasons. Rosh Hashanah is a New Year according to God's calendar. The Lord bestowed a New Year gift to the world on the 5th Day of Awe on September 25, 2017.

The Lord gave me a prophetic dream right during the High Holy Days; a message to believers and unbelievers about the momentous events that are about to occur in the future.

On Sunday night, September 25, 2017, I had a dream. This dream is about the great things about to incur on earth and in Heaven. I praise the Lord for still speaking to us by the power of His Holy Spirit. God gave me three messages in three parts of a dream.

Revival and Holy Spirit

First, I saw a downpour of heavy rain. We are in an area that is built uphill. Row houses and small buildings are on both sides of our street. I told my son and the people around me that I used to bathe in rainwater when I was a kid. My son went out and lay down on the street, enjoying the rain. The rainwater is flowing on this steep street in the likeness of a stream. The water is so clean that no one would mind bathing in it. As I was watching my son having fun in the rain, I saw a huge wave of water rushing from the bottom of the street rushing uphill with great force.

I instructed my son to hold tight for this wave when it passes over you. You will enjoy this bath if you choose to stay. He stayed at his spot to bathe in this strong wave of water rushing uphill.

Inside our lodging area, I saw a girl engrossed in sleep. She was unaware of her surroundings. She only wanted to sleep. The mosquitoes bite her, but she is so drunk in her sleep that she doesn't even care about missing this lifetime experience. I felt pity for her, seeing how mosquitoes continued biting her. My heart's desires to at least keep the mosquitoes away from her. Are the Esthers sleeping today?

God's Message of this Dream

In this dream, I am portrayed as a servant of God who is crying in the wilderness to prepare the way of the Lord. God's chosen servants in the Last Days are serving and ministering in the Spirit of Elijah. We are inviting people to come and receive the gifts of the Holy Spirit. The rain and stream of water flowing down the street symbolize the free and abundant supply of the Word of God and His Holy Spirit. I informed my son how good he would feel when taking a bath in rain showers. My son heard and went out to receive it. This symbolizes all those who are obedient to the voice of God, as His sheep hear His voice. They desire the gifts of the Holy Spirit, and they are taking a step of obedience to the will of the Lord. The children of God are soaked in the Holy Spirit . . . as it is available to all those who desire to receive it.

The gospel of salvation through Jesus Christ and the gift of the Holy Spirit has been provided to all the nations from the Day of Pentecost (early rain). It's been around us like a smooth stream of water flowing through the earth. It's coming from Heaven like smooth rain showers. But the next manifestation of the Holy Spirit on earth will be like a huge flood wave coming up forcefully (latter rain). I saw it coming towards us. I guided my son to be prepared for it. It is coming with a great power. The good news is that the promise of the Lord given in the Scriptures for this time and season is ready to be fulfilled. You will receive blessings out of the Heavenly Realm beyond your imagination. The outpour of the Holy Spirit is for those who are His obedient remnant.

A Move of God

We have witnessed the great working power of the Holy Spirit in the season of early rain—from the Day of Pentecost until now. But the "Latter Day Rain" coming on earth is going to be an epic occurrence. The Lord showed me the scale of both showers of rain in my dream. The next wave of the Holy Spirit that is ready to come on earth is going to be much greater than what mankind experienced in the past. A great number of signs and wonders, healings and miracles, and deliverance from demonic strongholds shall be witnessed. The revival will burst forth everywhere. Heaven and earth will shake by the power of the Holy Spirit.

> *It will come about after this that I will pour out My Spirit on all mankind; and your sons and daughters will prophesy, your old men will dream dreams, your young men will see visions. And even on the male and female servants I will pour out My Spirit in those days.* (Joel 2:28-29 NASB)

The gifts of the Holy Spirit are coming to you like a rushing wind, like a mighty stream of rainfall, like lightning, like a mighty fire proceeding from the Throne of God. Are you ready to receive this gift just like a son portrayed in my dream bathing in the rainfall and staying in the supernatural move of the wave uphill—this wave moved from the bottom of the street to the top of the hill? This portrays the mighty move of God supernaturally over and above the natural human expectations.

A lukewarm Church and unbelievers are portrayed as a sleeping girl in my dream. She will not wake up no matter what. All those who are engrossed in their sleep shall miss this great blessing of the Lord. They are slumbering and do not care about God and His salvation. They are asleep and lost in the cares of the world. They are enslaved to worldly pleasures. They suffer from the burden of the world and its slavery . . . but still sleeping and unbelieving of the Word of

God and the testimonies of His servants. In my dream, I pitied this girl bitten by mosquitoes . . . who is suffering at the hands of principalities and powers of darkness. But she is still asleep, not waking up to encounter God's presence and experience the redemptive power of the Holy Spirit to be delivered from the oppression of evil and darkness symbolized by being bitten by mosquitoes. God is, indeed, calling His daughters in these last days to wake up and join His army.

Birth Pains and Coming of the LORD

In the second part of my dream, I am discerning in the spirit that earth is ready to experience its birth pains, and I am pronouncing that. I am standing in an open field along with many others. As we were standing there, I saw the blue sky transforming more beautiful, brighter, clearer, and brilliant. I pointed it out and asked others if they saw it, too, and they did. It felt like a streak of glory light penetrating the sky and moving from our right to the left. As I was looking at the sky, I saw a lion walking as a majestic king at the height of clouds. The Lion was leading a great number of royalties dressed in imperial attires of brilliant colors and designs, dressed for a great royal ceremony. This innumerable number of people coming down towards us from heaven to earth were in the likeness of a huge caravan. The glory and brilliance of this majestic Lion caused the color of the sky to turn into a glorious sapphire and turquoise blue. It seems like they can see the change in the color of the sky, but they cannot see the Lion. I also told them that it was the glorious light of the Lord that changed the sky.

God's message of this Dream

In this part of my dream, I am discerning the birth pains on earth that the Lord Jesus Christ spoke about before His second coming on earth. The Bible talks about such birth pains.

> *For nation shall rise against nation, and kingdom against kingdom: and there shall be famines, and pestilences, and earthquakes, in divers places. All these are the beginning of sorrows.* (Matt. 24:7-8 KJV)

In my dream, I am not silent but sharing the message of the Lord about the fast-approaching birth pains, sufferings, and tribulations of the earth with everyone. I am helping the listeners to repent and seek salvation in the Messiah, the Lord Jesus Christ. All His servants are busy preparing the way of the Lord.

Yes, we are experiencing birth pains on earth. Conflicts between nations, famine, earthquakes, disasters, tsunamis, and floods are intensifying just like the birth pains a woman experiences. Her contractions grow stronger with a shorter span before delivery. Doctors tell an expecting mother to come to a hospital for delivery when contractions are about five minutes apart. Similarly, as we come nearer to the coming of the Lord, these birth pains at the earth's surface, and to its deep will grow more frequent and stronger. Sufferings and troubles will arise.

Alas, there still are many who continue to deny God and His Word.

> *Hypocrites! You can discern the face of the sky and of the earth, but how is it you do not discern this time?* (Luke 12:56)

I am amazed to see this Lion walking majestically in the sky. My eyes cannot leave His sight. I know the Lion is accompanied by royalties, but I am lost looking at the Lion and His majesty. I cannot describe this Lion; so elegant, so royal, and so majestic. He walks like a king. One cannot relate this Lion to the lions we have on earth.

Yeshua, the Lord Jesus Christ, is the offspring of David—the Lion of Judah. The Lion I saw in the Heavenly realm is the Lord Jesus Christ, also the morning star.

> *"I, Jesus, have sent My angel to testify to you these things in the churches. I am the Root and the Offspring of David, the Bright and Morning Star."* (Rev. 22:16)

> *But one of the elders said to me, "Do not weep. Behold, the Lion of the tribe of Judah, the Root of David, has prevailed to open the scroll and to loose its seven seals."* (Rev. 5:5)

My prophetic dream is a revelation for all believers in *Yeshua*—the Messiah to be comforted. Keep your eyes on the Lord Jesus Christ and look up to the Heavens with hope, as your redemption draws nigh.

> *For the Lord Himself will descend from heaven with a shout, with the voice of an archangel, and with the trumpet of God. And the dead in Christ will rise first. Then we who are alive and remain shall be caught up together with them in the clouds to meet the Lord in*

the air. And thus, we shall always be with the Lord. (1 Thess. 4:16-17)

Left Behind Persecuting Unbelievers

Third, I saw a man sitting in his black car. He looked angry about the experiences we were talking about. He threatened to hurt us or file a complaint against us.

God's message of this Dream

I discern in the spirit that his intention is evil against us. This man represents those scoffers who hate God and His will and live a relaxed deceptive lifestyle. They are blinded and can't see or understand the transformation of the heavens and earth. They are slumbering in their worldly pleasures. I saw this man wanting to hurt all those waiting for their King—the Lion of Judah. Therefore, we need to be ready for hate and persecution by those who are ungodly on this earth.

The third part of my dream is reflecting on the children of God standing in harvested fields, seeking the signs in Heaven and Earth. They are the faithful and obedient of the Lord who are not sitting, relaxing, or sleeping but are standing and observing the signs of the End Times, and the promise of His coming. A person who is standing is ready to go, ready to accomplish, ready to receive, ready to act, and ready for their redemption. Are you ready?

> *Then the sign of the Son of Man will appear in heaven, and then all the tribes of the earth will mourn, and they will see the Son of Man coming on the clouds of heaven with power and great glory.* (Matt. 24:30)

Therefore, do not be afraid, but like a good servant focus on His promises as His promises are ready to be fulfilled. Rejoice and receive your spiritual gifts that He is ready to pour out on the earth."

God who knows the end from the beginning, reveals the hidden things to His servants. Surely the Lord God does nothing unless He reveals His secrets to His servants the prophets.

In my first part of the dream, the Lord is preparing us to receive the outpouring of the latter-day rain prophesized in Joel 2:28-29. The second part of the dream is making us aware that the second coming of the Lord draws near as prophesized in Joel 2:30-31.

The last part of my prophetic dream is a word from the Lord: "Do not be discouraged and dismayed when you see the troubles, signs, and wonders in Heaven and on Earth. Look above to see the King of Judah for your redemption is near. He and His royal priesthood are drawing nigh. He is standing at the door of the Heavenly Realm ready to come." Come soon King Jesus!

"I Am Coming Quickly"

> *He who testifies to these things says, "Surely I am coming quickly." Amen. Even so, come, Lord Jesus!* (Rev. 22:20)

> *So Jesus answered and said to them, "Assuredly, I say to you, if you have faith and do not doubt, you will not only do what was done to the fig tree, but also if you say*

to this mountain, *'Be removed and be cast into the sea,'* it will be done. And whatever things you ask in prayer, believing, you will receive.* (Matthew 21:21-22)

PRAYER:

My Father in Heaven, my Lord, and my King! I worship You from the depths of my heart. You are my Shepherd, Redeemer, Sanctifier, Healer, Refuge, and Salvation. I enter into Your holy presence with humility of heart, hope of Your loving grace, and fear of Your righteous justice. I praise You Lord for the sacrifice of Your only begotten Son Jesus who is a perfect lamb of God to provide eternal life, salvation, hope, and healing for me and my house. Truly, You are worthy of all the honor, praises, and glory.

Lord, I pray in the name of Your precious Son Jesus to sanctify me and my house to be transformed into Your likeness to serve and to love. Lord, as we are living in times like the "Days of Noah," I pray, separate me and my house from the world and the things of the world just like Noah. Help us to hear Your will as Noah could hear Your instructions. Give us the gift of discernment so that we may not be deceived by the deceptions and lies of this world and its ruler, the devil.

Fill our hearts with thirst and hunger for Your Word, Your wisdom, and Your presence in our lives. Empower us with the power of the Holy Spirit. Bless me and my house to serve You, and be the partaker of the pour down of the "Latter Day Rains."

Lord, we pray for the peace of Jerusalem. Lord, protect Your church, Your servants, and Your elect from all snares of Satan. Lord, cast out every mountain erected against our ministry and everything that concerns us into the sea. Lord, make all mountains plain, not by might, nor by power, but by Your Holy Spirit power in our lives.

Our Father in Heaven, we pray this prayer in the precious Name of our Messiah, Yeshua – the Lord Jesus Christ!

Amen.

CHAPTER 7 by MK Henderson

READY TO WAR—ROOT OUT ENEMY, STRUCTURES, AND DECEPTION

The virgins in the parable found in Matthew chapter 25 who were caught without sufficient oil were deceived into thinking the bridegroom had delayed his coming. Perhaps a spirit of procrastination had come upon them and lulled them to sleep.

How does one avoid being deceived? Discernment is one of the keys. How does one gain discernment? We begin by praying for God to give us the gift of discerning of spirits. From the time I was a child I had a measure of prophetic discernment. There were certain things that I just knew by the Spirit of God.

As I matured in my walk with God, I developed more discernment. When God moved me to a third world country, I soon discovered that I did not have enough discernment. I began earnestly praying for more discernment and asked others to pray the same for me.

Over time my discernment level began to rise, and I began discerning many things, especially various types of spirits, good and bad, that were operating in people and the atmosphere around me.

I was living in a part of the world where people naturally have a heightened sense of awareness of the spiritual realm. As children growing up, they are taught to operate in the spiritual realm at a very young age, whether for good or evil.

Many of these people arrive in the US still practicing what they learned as children. They hate it that God sends people to their home countries to evangelize with the Gospel of Jesus Christ, and they do all they can to stop them. Many will even join churches and prayer groups to work against God's people. They slyly work their beliefs into prayer meetings and or Bible study groups, and soon people are believing and accepting what they have to say. Others join churches to sow discord and bring confusion from within.

One group, for instance, was taught they should not go into the world to preach the gospel as it is not proper to go into another country and try to change the culture to a Christ-like culture. This Bible study group conformed to the belief of the spy, the infiltrator. Because these Hindus and Buddhists knew how to use Christanese—typical Christian phrases and catchwords, they were readily accepted as believers in Jesus.

Muslim young men have been instructed to go into college campuses to join the Christian clubs and gradually change the beliefs of the club members. One former Muslim publicly confessed that was his mandate when sent to the USA. He was to convince the Christian students they worshiped the same God.

I heard this man speak at a public event when he explained the settled way they are trained to work. He said the goal was to marry American women and make Muslim babies and soon they would outnumber the natural born Americans in the country.

One must pray for discernment as there are many signs, wonders, and apparitions out there. One day a young man requested of one of my indigenous pastors the use of his church facility. He was granted the use of the church by a pastor or leader. He explained that he would be displaying healings and miracles that day.

I attended, as I felt that something may be amiss. He was introduced on the platform by a well-known pastor who had become involved in a cult. He was snatched into the cult seeking financial gain, which they gave, to help his church.

The young man asked those who needed healing to come forward and he would pray for them. I noticed that when he prayed there were demonic manifestations, but he was not casting them out in the name of Jesus. He was just commanding the demons to be quiet. Some other strange phenomenon appeared, and I knew it was not the Holy Spirit operating.

Later, after he finished, the pastor who introduced him asked him to do a radio interview of the miracles he claimed to have performed. He was eager to do that. Later, when I asked him if the lead pastor there and I could pray for him, he declined and was fearful of us praying for him or even touching him.

Later I asked the lead pastor what he thought was happening, and he said he thought that it was not an operation of the Holy Spirit. The young man conducting the meeting later called me and requested I join his team traveling to various places to perform miracles. He also informed me he spoke over one hundred tongues and was quite proud of that. The devil also has people speaking in tongues in Satanic churches in the USA and other countries.

When I pointed out to him phenomena that was not biblical, using Scripture, he became resentful. He refused to have his eyes opened and later admitted that he had been a part of the same cult as the pastor who had introduced him that day. Thank God the pastor of my church had not encouraged any of his people to attend, and only three of us were there to try the spirit and see if God was in it.

Earlier that same day, when I was preaching in that same church building, we had a powerful move of the Holy Spirit and people were touched by the power of God. Some received the baptism of the Holy Spirit as described in Acts chapter 3, and others were healed instantly by God's power. Some people we didn't even lay hands on. God just touched them and they were healed and delivered where they sat worshipping!

How does one recognize those lying signs and wonders? How does one recognize a counterfeit believer? My mentor, Barbara Wentroble, explains in her book *Removing the Veil of Deception,* published by Chosen. In these last days women of God must increase their spiritual discernment and accuracy every day.

Discerning of spirits is the supernatural gift of the Holy Spirit. It is the supernatural gift that we use to identify the source of the spiritual force influencing an event, circumstances, atmosphere of a place or around a person and even your own thoughts.

God can give discernment at any time and any place to any believer when needed. We get to know God through His Word and through the Holy Spirit speaking in our hearts. How does one avoid being deceived? Discernment is the key. How does one gain discernment besides praying for God to give the gift of discerning of spirits? The Word of

God also brings revelation. His word is a lamp unto our feet. Many times, God speaks to us, and we just know something is not right, so we pray and ask the Holy Spirit to bring revelation as to what is happening.

God also speaks and gives us revelation through dreams. God has always spoken to me through dreams and the last few years even more so, giving me the interpretation as soon as I wake up. Sometimes I consult others to get a broader interpretation of a dream.

Don't let others tell you that you are paranoid because you sense things and hear from the Lord. We must keep our spiritual ears sharp and not write off what we hear as our imagination, but ask God about what we are experiencing or sensing.

I have noticed nowadays there is much deception infiltrating the body of Christ with people coming in with Hindu, Buddhist, and New Age beliefs and practices which they integrate into their Christian beliefs and encourage others to do the same using "Christian" lingo. Unfortunately, most in the body of Christ do not have the discernment to even be aware that those they consider their Christian "believing" friends are in reality non-believers to Jesus. They don't even know him! They only "know" the works of darkness they have learned to practice.

Some churches hire event planners for their conferences and are focused on their expertise. They fail to see the spiritual aspect of the person and submit themselves to them. As a result, their ministries are compromised as they have hired New Age practitioners unaware. We must pray about all decisions, especially those involving and affecting other believers.

We must re-claim our territory and nations for Jesus. We must seek God for our role and confirm it so we can be confident, knowing who we are and knowing our God is mighty and able to save, deliver, heal, and restore. We are in the world but not of it. We must come out of Babylon, the evil system. We must be set apart for the Lord.

> *And I heard another voice from heaven saying, Come out of her, my people, that ye be not partakers of her sins, and that ye receive not of her plagues. For her sins have reached unto heaven, and God hath remembered her iniquities.* (Rev.18:4-5 KJV)

PRAYER:

Lord, open our eyes and make us sensitive to Your Holy Spirit. Help us to rely more on the Holy Spirit and less on human reasoning. Lord, increase our gift of discernment so that we may discern truth from falsehood. Lord, direct us, and give us a greater desire for more of Your Holy Spirit and for all of the gifts of the Spirit. Help us go forth in Your power and anointing. Give us words of knowledge and increase us in wisdom and understanding.

Chapter 8 by MK Henderson and Donna Schambach

READY TO BUILD THE KINGDOM IN MIRACLES, SIGNS, AND WONDERS

MK Henderson:

Since 1999 God has been sending me to the nations that are kingdoms with a king; a Himalayan Mt. kingdom and a kingdom in the South Pacific Islands.

As believers, we must understand the definition of a kingdom to fully understand what God is wanting us to learn about manifesting His kingdom on earth as Jesus did when He walked here. This is especially important for warrior women to understand.

A kingdom is a domain, a place that is ruled and governed by a king who has dominion and authority to influence the will and minds of people to produce a certain culture in His kingdom.

Jesus didn't come to bring religion as it was already on the earth as the scribes and Pharisees were operating in it under the law of Moses.

God wants His church to go from "religion" and the "law" or "institutional Christianity" to His kingdom. Emperor Constantine introduced religious rituals into the church when he partnered with the pagan worship of the goddess Ishtar (from which the word Easter originates). He forbid believers to celebrate Passover which God ordered them to celebrate in remembrance of their coming out of Egypt and crossing the Red Sea.

Today we see a Christian sub-culture that doesn't reflect Christ's kingdom. In the kingdom of God there isn't overwhelming strife, sickness, hate, poverty, etc. Jesus wants His people to see the manifestations on earth of His kingdom of heaven.

> *But Jesus said unto them, They need not depart, give ye them to eat. And they said unto him, We have here but five loaves, and two fishes. He said, Bring them hither to me. And he commanded the multitude to sit down on the grass, and took the five loaves, and the two fishes, and looking up to heaven, he blessed, and brake, and gave the loaves to his disciples, and the disciples to the multitude. And they did all eat, and were filled: and they took up the fragments that remained twelve baskets full.* (Matt.14:16-21 KJV)

Peter had to catch a fish to retrieve the coin to pay His taxes, and the loaves and fishes multiplied. This is the kingdom of God at work, doing miracles, signs, and wonders.

My friends and I have also seen God make money multiply in our hands unexpectedly. Some people say God doesn't have money in heaven to send down to us. I laugh, as I've discovered that God gives to us in unexpected ways and in unexpected times. Most of the time He uses other people to give to us. Other times He tests our faith, like telling Peter to go fishing to get the money to pay his taxes. We must learn to trust God completely for all of our needs.

The kingdom of God is governed by God. He rules. He also desires for us to rule the earth so it can be a replica of the kingdom of God in heaven. The original plan with Adam and Eve was to rule the earth and take dominion. So must we do as well. The glory of God takes over the atmosphere through us. Jesus established the kingdom of God to rule on the earth through us. I saw signs saying "for the kingdom" as I traveled in the Pacific Islands. All the people working together for the kingdom.

Kingdoms can be conquered by enemies on the outside as well as enemies within who have their own agendas. People of the kingdom must prevent an invasion. The king must be alert to protect the kingdom citizens at all times. The devil lies to the citizens of God's kingdom. We, as kings and priests, are to rule the spiritual atmosphere around us. God's glory goes where we go. We carry His presence.

God has given each of us a seat in His kingdom; a seat of power and authority. We are surrounded by angelic guards who act as security court officers, always on duty when we call them. They are on their watch lest we dash our foot against a stone.[29] As the bride of Christ, the "queen," our seat goes with us everywhere we go.

While I was visiting one particular country, a kingdom governed by a king and queen, I had the honor of having the queen in the audience I was addressing. When she arrived, her guard carried in her seat, on which she sat, a seat of royalty and authority. At the end of the meeting, within minutes after she left, a palace guard came in and retrieved her seat. My hostess exclaimed, "Oh, he forgot to take the seat with her." Obviously that seat upon which she sits goes with her everywhere she goes because it is a symbol of the royal position in which she sits.

In the kingdom of God our seat of authority and power goes with us everywhere we go as it is our position in the kingdom. In this place, the queen's security also protected her vehicle even when she was not in it, not allowing anyone near it. Angels guard my house and vehicle also to keep the enemy from encroaching upon me. I thank Jesus, my Bridegroom King, for my position in the kingdom of God.

Later in this chapter, my friend, evangelist Donna Schambach, illustrates how our seat functions, even in Maasailand, Kenya. She has told me stories of how angels went before her in precarious situations and protected her.

There is a spiritual war and a cultural war between the kingdom of God and the kingdom of darkness. In some cultures, people worship the dead and idols. Believers have difficult lives in those cultures, yet they show the kingdom of God! I've seen the dead raised, lame walk, and deaf hear. FAITH is the currency of the kingdom of God!

We seek to impact the seven mountains of cultural influence everywhere we go. They are: education, government, family, church, entertainment, business, and media. God opens the doors for us to be able to influence these areas of culture. Amen!

"I want to be a child of the Kingdom, living in paradise—walking with Jesus every day. We won't give up the fight! It will be such a beautiful day when He calls my name because we walk in victory!' The words of this popular island song still ring in my ears. Yes, it's all about the Kingdom of God. A sign got my attention: "Bread for the Kingdom! Jesus is the bread of life!"

The kingdoms of this earth are to become the kingdoms of our God, a replica of the kingdom of God! Yes!

"'The battle lines have been drawn, and I've called you up to a higher place to see both sides. Proclaim My name, and choose your side. I'm calling light bearers to rise up and follow Me into the dark places because darkness can't cancel the light. I'm placing the enforcement of My kingdom in your voice. Today the toothless lion has died. My kingdom lives inside of you, and you will roar. Don't be afraid of the enforcement of My kingdom. Enforce My rule in the earth,' says the Lord."[30]

Donna J. Schambach, Evangelist, Revivalist

It was summer in Maasailand, Kenya, and the women and children of the Maasai community had been left behind by their husbands who went out in search of water for their livestock and, of course, for their families.

I was part of a missions group who came to install a well and preach the Gospel to this most colorful and beautiful people group. We understood that the region was in drought as it hadn't rained for almost a year. The wells were going dry, and the cattle were dying. The drought was taking a toll on their humble economy and on their bodies.

My night to minister was Day #4 of the crusade. I had less than an hour to preach and then leave the platform because the buses that brought us were rolling out early.

As I left the hotel to go and preach to the Maasai folks, the Lord prompted my spirit to take a beautiful red cloth someone had given me. It had been woven by the Maasai tribe. I had no idea why the Lord wanted me to take it, but I would come to find out in the middle of my message, "The Living Water."

Using two different passages, one from Genesis 26 and the other from John 4, I spoke about my God who supplies both water for our physical needs and water for our spiritual needs. Genesis 26 is all about Isaac who was going down to Egypt for help in the time of drought and famine. On the way, God told him to stay in Gerar, and Isaac was obedient. More than that, Isaac began to dig and plant in that land, and God gave him a 100-fold increase in the first year. God's water supply is always more than enough!

Then I spoke about the Samaritan woman who was sitting at a well in the heat of the day, when Jesus came to her for a visit. He started the conversation by asking for water. She was stunned that this Jewish man was talking to her, a Samaritan woman, asking her for water. (The Samaritans were a mixed-race group and looked down upon by the Jews.) Jesus told this woman something that would completely revolutionize her world!

> *"If you knew the gift of God and who it is that asks you for a drink, you would have asked him and he would have given you living water."* (John 4:10 NIV)

Well, not only did that woman take a big drink of the Living Water, she ran back to her village to share it with everyone she knew. Something HUGE had happened to her soul!

What happened next in Maasailand became a sign to all who were hearing the Word of God. God had me take the beautiful red Maasai cloth and hold it up in front of the entire tribe. In fact, I asked the pastor to hold one end and a missionary to hold the other. I instructed the people, when I had those men lift the cloth in the air, they were to praise

God at the top of their lungs—thanking Him for living water and natural water.

You should have heard the shouting! Oh, you should have seen the jumping. (The Maasai are known for their vertical jumping, and some can get 5' off the ground!)

As we lifted the cloth, seven times in total, the praise of the people became louder and more boisterous. It was a sight to behold. I gave the altar call, and many came to receive Jesus as Savior and Lord. Then, we had to swiftly head to the buses.

On that bus, I will always remember, we began to see clouds form in the skies behind us. We heard thunder—and then the rains began to fall. The missionaries told us the rains did not stop for 7 days. It was a sign to those precious Maasai that God had heard their cries!

I tell this story because it illustrates just how much God wants to get the story of His unmatched love to hungry and thirsty people.

Through the years, I have been privileged to see God perform outstanding miracles through the ministry of my father, R.W. Schambach, and also through mine. So many deaf ears opened. So many rising out of wheelchairs. Blind eyes open—cancer victims, healed. A man who could see out of a glass eye, after prayer, and a woman who could drink for the first time, without an esophagus—instantaneous miracles of God who put His mighty power on display!

Why are miracles important for our ministries? Miracles lift the heavy burdens of the downtrodden. Miracles restore hope to the destitute. Miracles convey the compassion of a loving Father who sent His only Son to this earth to free us from our sin.

The Apostle Paul spoke about their importance in conveying the Gospel message:

> *And my speech and my preaching was not with enticing words of man's wisdom, but in demonstration of the Spirit and of power: That your faith should not stand in the wisdom of men, but in the power of God.* (1 Cor. 2:4-5 KJV)

He knew the Holy Ghost was poured out upon believers with power—spiritual dynamite—to blow up the strongholds of the kingdom of evil. We who know Christ and minister for Him must be filled with the Holy Spirit and demonstrate the power of God as we proclaim His Word.

For a greater understanding of how to function in this way, you may want to consider picking up my book, **The Anointing For Miracles,** at **schambach.org** It is filled with miracle testimonies and chronicles my journey into a miracle ministry as the Holy Spirit taught me.

PRAYER:

Dear Lord Jesus,

Help me to obey and go wherever You send me and to see You work in miraculous ways. I desire to see blind eyes open, deaf ears hear, the lame walk, and the dead raised for Your glory! Use me for Your honor and glory! Amen.

Chapter 9 by MK Henderson

READY TO FACE THE WAR WITH NEW STRATEGIES

Too often, when people see someone in warfare, they immediately think that person is having problems or is enduring difficulties because she is in sin. Unfortunately, this myth is creating many problems for women warriors because instead of praying for them people are assuming they are in sin. The enemy doesn't waste time attacking people whom he already has in his grip of sin and whom he is using against the Lord's soldiers in the battles.

The Bible says those who serve the Lord with all their heart, soul, and mind will suffer as Jesus suffered. It is not usually because they are in sin, but because they have just won a great battle in the Lord and the evil one is mad and is trying to cause a backlash. Where are those prayer warriors who should be praying for you? Sometimes those who are to be your covering forget to pray for you so one must remind them to pray. Other times those who are your covering are having to fight their own battle at the same time you are going through your battle.

God's army has ranks like any other army. A private cannot begin planning battle strategies and giving orders as he has never been in a war before. That is the job of the general who has fought in many wars and used various winning strategies. He knows from experience what works and what doesn't work.

It is unfortunate that many privates do not have a teachable spirit and desire a higher rank immediately, to impress others rather than being eager to learn from the seasoned generals. I have had the same mentor for nearly twenty years, and she is a seasoned general. She lives her life by practicing what she teaches. These type of mentors are very valuable and should be respected and honored with loyalty. My mentor is also open to what I am suggesting and hearing from the Lord.

Know who is in your battalion and who is fighting with you. Are they all YES people or do they have ideas and insight to share with you to build a better war strategy? These strategies must always be based on the Word of God which never fails.

Good battle strategies must encourage courage and discourage fear in the ranks among the troops. Sometimes great strategies will involve risk. That's where faith comes in.

In the Bible we see many strategies for battle in the Old Testament and the New Testament as well. All of these strategies required faith activation. We must overcome our fears with faith. One of my favorite verses is Isaiah 41:10, which I recite every morning.

> *"Fear not, for I am with you; be not dismayed, for I am your God. I will strengthen you, yes I will help you, I will uphold you with my with My righteous right hand."*

Jesus is our Commander in chief. He is *for* us and *with* us as we follow His plan. Sometimes He allows us to be in crisis situations to overcome our fears and become fearless on a particular level. Once we have conquered that fear then He trains us in a higher level of warfare to conquer a whole new level of fear, so we can fulfill God's plan for our destiny and future.

We qualify because our Bridegroom King has extended the scepter and chosen us. So we must not disqualify ourselves or allow others to disqualify us.

Esther hesitated to get involved but prayed about the dilemma facing the Jews. As she prayed and fasted, God gave her the strategy to begin to solve the problem and save the lives of her people.[31]

Esther requested that Mordecai direct the people to fast and pray. It is very important to have intercessors praying for you. Nowadays it may be difficult to find people who are serious about prayer so ask God to send you praying people.

For several years I was in situations where people were coming against me and trying to sabotage God's work and even put my life in danger. I kept praying for more intercessors as I only had a few, not even enough to cover me 24/7! One day God put me in contact with a prayer group who had been remembering me in prayer regularly, although I knew nothing about them. Most of them didn't even know me but were praying for me regularly as their prayer group leader directed them. My situation began to change, and I became stronger in my spirit.

Esther waited upon God to move forward and then when she knew the time was right she went to the palace in confidence.

God will use many women as Esthers to go before high-level government leaders. While in a third world country, the Lord led me to begin praying for a woman leader and informed me that one day I would meet her. In fact, a few months after I began praying for this woman, God arranged a divine appointment with her and gave me favor with her. She invited me into her home to share a meal with her friends and family. In this culture that is a big event! During dinner they asked me about my faith and were genuinely interested in having their questions answered. One of her family members had been studying the Torah.

A year later God prepared me for a second meeting with this woman. He gave me a prophetic word for her and told me to dress as an ambassador to go and meet her. I requested the meeting, and it was granted. I also was instructed by the Lord to bring a gift as one always should have a gift when meeting royalty.

There were subsequent meetings in which the protocol was the same. After years of meeting once or twice annually, I asked Jesus to go to her and be with her during a crisis in which she was fighting for her life. The next time I saw her, a few months later, she informed me that Jesus had come to her, and she knew she was now a child of God. God does above and beyond what we can do or think! So speak the impossible and believe God.

Women, we are, indeed, a part of the royal priesthood, as Jesus made the way for us to sit with Him in heavenly places and even enter the holy of holies because His blood covers us. We are coming into the kingdom for such a time as this in the last dispensation.

I believe He will give us wealth to influence this generation through media and other avenues. We must not be afraid to expose evil and become truth bearers. God needs us as His authority here on the earth, and He has validated you. You are complete in Him, and not limited by time or space.[32]

Because of where we sit, we can be confident of victory and can cause the enemy to flee. If you have taken a break, in the Lord's timing, be ready to get back in the battle for souls. The Lord is with you mighty woman of God. And there can be joy in the war. God does have a sense of humor! It gives hope in the heat of the war.

Recently I had been in high level warfare during a very long season. God showed me what the devil meant for bad He could turn for good. After intense warfare one night, the Lord gave me a vision of a pair of heavy combat boots. They were bronze and made of leather and steel. Then the Lord said, "You have just been promoted!"

I was stunned because I felt I had been fighting alone. Jesus was with me! Then He added, "Kick the enemy from KTM to Timbuktu! He was cheering and supporting me. The bronze combat boots represented power, wisdom, and compassion. The Lord was assuring me He had given me all those attributes.

When the heavens are opened over us and we become one with the Holy Spirit, the works of Satan have no place in our midst because the kingdom of God is with us! Wherever the Spirit of God is poured out, there is no room left for the enemy to operate.[33]

Pay close attention to what we listen to as social media and secular news bombards us daily. Our words can bring joy in the war or depression and disappointment.

> *Not what goes into the mouth defiles a man; but what comes out of the mouth, this defiles a man."* (Matt 15:11)

As leaders, we're responsible to God for what comes out of our mouths. Jesus said it is not what goes into a man's mouth but what comes out that makes him unclean.

> *Those things which proceed out of the mouth come from the heart, and they defile a man. For out of the heart proceed evil thoughts, murders, adulteries, fornications, thefts, false witness, blasphemies.* (Matt. 15:18-19)

Our mouth is a reflection of the heart, and the heart produces all forms of evil, including false testimony. You can check your heart condition by listening to what comes out of your mouth, and the attitude behind your words. Both sin and repentance take place in the heart.[34]

We are also responsible for what we hear on many levels. While we may not be able to control what other people say, we can definitely control how we let the information affect our own hearts. It has been my experience that people, including leaders, often take a one-sided story or a partial truth and fill in the blanks without ever contacting the other parties involved. When this happens, it can allow the devil a foothold of accusation seeded by false testimony. False testimony can settle into our hearts and become our version of truth.

An example of that is what I experienced recently as I had given a Christian brother a money order to cash and take to my adopted country. After several weeks I hadn't heard if the other party had received the funds, so I contacted the brother and was informed he hadn't cashed it before he left the USA and I could try to get the funds refunded. I still had the receipt, so I returned to the outlet where it had been purchased. The employee of the outlet informed me that I had been scammed. I explained to her that I had not been scammed and the person just couldn't find a place to cash it before he went overseas. She repeated several times that I had been scammed. I insisted that I had not.

I went to another outlet to try to get a refund and on the way there the enemy kept telling me it was no use as I had been scammed. I ended up going to three places until I received my refund. By the way, my spirit went from being joyful that day to feeling down because of the words and declarations of the first person. The brother was new to my adopted country. He did not know he could cash it there and give to the intended recipient as instructed.

Another strategy is to overcome fear and recognize it for what it really is: False Evidence Appearing Real. Fear is actually a spirit, appearing real to our minds and emotions.

> *For God has not given us a spirit of fear, but of power and of love and of a sound mind.* (2 Tim. 1:7)

We must speak aloud and tell that spirit to go from us in Jesus' name and not return. We can also take communion and focus on Jesus and His blood that was shed for us. The enemy is fearful of the blood of Jesus.

During the fearful times in my life, I have stood on Psalm 91, repeating it daily. God will allow you to go to a place to address and confront your fears to make you stronger in certain areas of your life for the future. It's here that you learn to overcome the enemy by resting in the shadow of His wings. Jesus has overcome the enemy on the cross and our fight is against powers and principalities to enforce what Jesus has already done for us.

Instead of fear we have FAITH: Here is the acronym: Fearless spirit, Agreement with Jesus , Intimacy with Jesus, Tethered to Jesus, and Hearing Jesus's voice.

We can have joy because He has given a fearless spirit and we are in agreement with Jesus, one with him. We are in intimacy with and tethered to Jesus, listening to His voice, which is calming. I have made the following verses my weapons in the war.

> *His anger is but for a moment, His favor is for life; weeping may endure for a night, but joy comes in the morning. You have turned for me my mourning into dancing; You have put off my sackcloth and clothed me with gladness, to the end that my glory may sing praise to You and not be silent. Oh lord my God, I will give thanks to You forever.* (Ps. 30:5, 11-12)

> *"Then shall the virgin rejoice in the dance, and the young men and the old, together; for I will turn their mourning to joy, will comfort them, and make them rejoice rather than sorrow."* (Jer. 31:13)

> *"To console those who mourn in Zion, to give them beauty for ashes, the oil of joy for mourning, the garment of praise for spirit of heaviness; that they may be called trees of righteousness, the planting of the Lord, that He may be glorified."* (Isa. 61:3)

It is the Spirit of God that produces joy. It causes us to see the future, to rise above sorrow or loss.[35]

If the enemy can remove your joy, he can remove your strength. Strength is the ability to withstand our next attack.

Therefore, maintaining strength is key to our Spirit-filled life. Sorrow and joy are firmly linked. Perhaps it is because the deeper we experience sorrow the more capacity we have for joy. Although we may only see the sorrow and tears of the night, He has planned a bright and beautiful morning full of joy.

The Lord announces victory, and throngs of women shout the happy news . . . enemy kings and their armies flee while women divided the plunder.

> *The Lord gave the word; Great was the company of those who proclaimed it: "Kings of armies flee, they flee, and she who remains at home divides the spoil. Though you lie down among the sheepfolds, you will be like the wings of a dove covered with silver, and her feathers with yellow gold." When the Almighty scattered kings in it, it was white as snow in Zalmon."* (Ps. 68:11-14)

Yes, the battle is on. The war is raging, and we have already been declared the victor as the victory flag is waving high. Victory is here and now.

We speak NOW! We speak in faith as we're believing in God's Word, and we can just see Him doing above and beyond all that we ask or think.

In the book *Authority to Tread* (2005), Becca Greenwood defines spiritual warfare as an invisible battle in the spiritual realm involving a power confrontation between the kingdom of darkness and the kingdom of God.[36]

She describes three levels of warfare.

1) Ground level—breaking demonic influences in an individual (deliverance).
2) Occult level—opposition to a more, structured level of demonic authority such as witchcraft, freemasonry, new age, satanism, and eastern religions. Warfare prayer is required.
3) Strategic level—high ranking principalities and powers assigned to geographical areas and territories in a social network such as a government. An example of this level of warfare is described in the following scenario In Philippi, where a slave girl followed Paul and Silas.

And it came to pass, as we went to prayer, a certain damsel possessed with a spirit of divination met us, which brought her masters much gain by soothsaying: the same followed Paul and us, and cried, saying, These men are the servants of the most high God, which shew unto us the way of salvation. And this did she many days. But Paul, being grieved, turned and said to the spirit, I command thee in the name of Jesus Christ to come out of her. And he came out the same hour.

And when her masters saw that the hope of their gains were gone, they caught Paul and Silas and drew them into the marketplace unto the rulers. And brought them to the magistrates, saying, These men, being Jews, do exceedingly trouble our city. And teach customs, which are not lawful for us to receive, neither to observe, being Romans. And the multitude rose up together against them; and the magistrates rent off their clothes, and commanded to beat them. And when they had many stripes upon them, they cast them into prison, and made their feet fast in the stocks.

And at midnight Paul and Silas prayed, and sang praises unto God: and the prisoners heard them. And suddenly there was a great earthquake, so that the foundations of the prison were shaken: and immediately all the doors were opened, and every one's bands were loosed. (Acts 16:16-26 KJV)

When Paul ousted the territorial spirit operating through the slave girl, Paul and Silas were beaten and thrown into prison. The foundations of paganism are shaken when releasing the people from darkness.

For example, I prophesied about the shaking in the Himalayan Mts. during a 48-hour prayer meeting in a church in which about 2000 believers had gathered to pray and fast.

Only a few weeks later, a 7.9 earthquake hit the region and it was very widespread. I had read a Scripture about God dealing with the people who are stiff-necked and how he would cause a shaking. Large significant cultural buildings were the first to go down in the shaking. Aftershocks were reported for years!

For several years we had been meeting with intercessors from many locations and praying over the seven mountains of influence. Many prayed and fasted from 7 am to 7 pm every day for three weeks to see God move.

We had previously finished spiritual mapping, so we knew what the strongholds were that were working in the nations of the region. We had noted the ruling spirits over the region, and our intercession always coincided with pagan festivals that lasted a couple of weeks. Our prayer and fasting usually continued for 21 days.

After several years of this prayer and fasting routine, we witnessed a great victory as there was a sudden positive shifting in the political atmosphere of the region for the better.

PRAYER:

Thank you, Holy Spirit, for guiding and directing us and for ordering our steps as we enter this war and endure many battles for Your glory. We thank You, Jesus, for the finished work on Calvary that guarantees us the victory. We stand upon Your promises in Isaiah 54:17, that no weapon against us will succeed.

Chapter 10 by MK Henderson

READY TO REDEEM THE TIME FOR HARVEST AND REVIVAL

We must join up with what God is doing. His will is already in place. You can't fail. Partnering with God in His timing causes all things to line up and be in order. I've seen this happen for me on recent trips. In one country the hotel reservation was difficult to secure, due to it being tourist season. However, it all came together as soon as God revealed to me that I was to stay in a house instead of a hotel and have people come in to pray.

God showed me in advance who I would meet and the cities I would be traveling to as well as the churches God would give me access to minister in. It all happened just as God had revealed to me beforehand. Remember, when the enemy comes in like a flood, God will raise up a standard against him.

Prerequisites for Warfare:

As warriors, we stand in the authority of our blood covenant with Jesus. When we receive Jesus as our Savior, we confess our sins, repent, surrender, and submit to Him. "Come boldly to the throne of grace to obtain mercy and find grace to help in time of need" (Heb. 4:16 KJV).

As a college student, I recall the day I made Jesus Lord of my life. I knew He would direct me in my career, field of study, where I would live, who I would marry, and if I would marry. God would use my talents and gifts for His glory.

While living in New York City, the Lord Jesus called me to a life of spiritual warfare. At the time I only knew of one or two people who had accepted that kind of call. The Lord assured me that He would fight for me. At that time, I was being tested on every hand and God did fight for me! He was always with me and revealing more to be gained in my relationship with Him. Twenty years later in a foreign country, the Lord called me to a lifestyle of prayer as a priority. That didn't mean I didn't have struggles, but it enabled me to endure under the harshest circumstances and situations.

The Lord was teaching my hands to war and my fingers to fight.[37] Teaching me how to wear the full armor of God, watching my actions and words. Many times, I had to repent for incorrect words and actions. To experience the faithfulness of God, we must be faithful in our daily lives. In these last days God is testing our faith.

Over the years I have learned to sanctify my living areas by claiming the property or space for the Lord, whether land, house, garage, or vehicle. I cleanse and sanctify it using the blood of Jesus. I also removed unholy things like idols when living in a foreign country. In one of my rentals the owners stored idols in a worship room on top of the house. I had to take those things to the owner's family for them to do with them as they pleased. I could not keep them in my living area, nor could I burn them as they belonged to another person.

One should be careful of accepting gifts from idol worshippers as well. One homeowner gave me a beautiful garment, however I never felt comfortable to wear it so I never did. She was a dedicated idol worshipper. I ended up removing it from my closet.

Practice Psalm 51 often. The Holy Spirit will remove any and all sin as we inquire of Him to do so.

Do not fraternize with rebellious people claiming to be children of God. Rebellion is as the sin of witchcraft. (I Sam. 15:23 KJV)

When you discern that the enemy has sent his agents to conduct rituals on your property, ask the Lord what and where the object or substance is that was brought onto your property. It must be removed. Before removing it, cover it with the blood of Jesus as Jesus blood makes null and void the work of Satan.

Walk your property boundaries and use anointing oil sanctifying your property in Jesus' name, speaking to your land, declaring that it not work against you in any way but only bring prosperity. Periodically, anoint all windows, doors, and openings in your house with holy anointing oil.

We are living in a new era of spiritual authority for women. It is also a time for women to come together in groups or networks in intercession like never before. We need each other and we need the corporate anointing.

Unprecedented evil has been released in recent years in the nations on a large scale, even in the United States of America, in rural and urban areas. Even in places where there are only a few believers, try to establish a unity in purpose and prayer. It helps us to hear God more clearly and keeps us from acting on impulse.

Jesus sent out two by two. Sometimes it's not possible to have a second person, especially if you are in a rural area with few believers. When traveling to another destination I always make contact with mature believers ahead of time at my destination, so they are already praying for me and ready to join the ministry upon my arrival in prayer and intercession.

I also have a spiritual covering from a couple of other ministries; I seek input from them in decision making. For married women, their husbands are their spiritual covering. Husband and wife should seek input from each other in making decisions, especially involving ministry.

It is good to converse with the Holy Spirit throughout the day as He will assist you, if you ask Him. He is always reminding me of small things and details that I may forget. For years I have begun my day communicating with the Lord in prayer, worship, and reading His Word. This sets my mind, will, and emotions for the day. It makes me sensitive to the voice of the Holy Spirit. I may make mistakes during the day, but the Holy Spirit quickens me, and I can redo something and make it right.

This is especially true when speaking verbally in conversations or in written emails and text messages. Our words are spirit so we must work on guarding our tongues. As God's mouthpiece, many times we don't realize the weight our words carry in the spirit realm and the affect they have on others. Ask the Holy Spirit to make you sensitive in this area. He will nudge or prompt you if you over spoke due to being overcome with emotions.

Arthur Matthews was living in China (1938-1949) when communism took over. He and his family were under house arrest for four years. He says, "We tend to look at the circumstances of life in terms of what they may do to our cherished hopes and convenience, and we shape our decisions and reactions accordingly. When problems threaten, we rush to God, not to see His perspective, but to ask Him to deflect the trouble. Our self-concern takes priority over what it is God might be trying to do through the trouble."[38]

He prayed,

Oh, Lord, help us not to be a part of this generation that sees security and prosperity as evidence of God's blessing. Let us see suffering as a path to greater intimacy with You, Lord.

Amen

PRAYER:

Dear, Lord, We know that You are calling women to be active soldiers in this end time army to see Your plan fulfilled on this earth. Help us to endure hardship as a good soldier. We know You promised to be with us always.

Summary by MK Henderson

In a dream the Lord gave me, I realized how important the church mountain is in these last days. In the dream I was standing next to the Matterhorn, the mother of mountains in the Swiss Alps. However, I was standing on a white floorboard. The Matterhorn began to slip and slide, and I reached out to sturdy it. You see, the Matterhorn was also my stability, and when it began to slip and slide, I also became unsteady. The white board I was standing on began to slide, and I saw underneath a sea of water. The sea is referred to as people (nations) in the prophetic. Then the Lord said to me, "The waters which you saw, where the harlot sits, are peoples, multitudes, nations, and tongues" (Rev. 17:15).

In Micah 4:1 it says that in the last days the mountain of the Lord's temple will be established. Out of the seven mountains: of influence, government, education, business, entertainment, media, family, and the church, the mountain of the Lord's temple will be established as the highest of these mountains. That means the "church" will be exalted high above the hills and the people will stream to it. God desires the last days church to be the one with the greatest influence in society.

God has positioned me and other women in a position to keep the "church" mountain from slipping and sliding so that we can stand over the lost souls on the white board, in purity and holiness, clean before the Lord. The church mountain gives stability to a society. We are to stand in a position of holiness and purity. We must return the "church" mountain to its rightful place as it has been slipping and sliding, unstable. The church mountain must be in its rightful place in the hearts, souls, and spirits of the people. When this happens, the church will be exalted and the people will stream to the temple of God, the mountain of God. When I say "temple," or "Church," I'm not referring to a building but to the people of God that are united in Christ.

This dream is about my position and role in these last days. It is also about your role as women warriors. May God give us wisdom, knowledge, understanding, and discernment in these perilous times, so that we may be able to lead people to their place in Him!

Now I am going to talk a little about the church or ecclesia. There is so much misunderstanding about the "church" nowadays! First, we see in the book of Acts a model of what the church really is . . . a united body of believers with the fear of God, genuine love of Jesus, and willingness to do for each other as displayed in sacrifices made for one another.

Unfortunately, much of the church in America doesn't look like the "church" we see in the book of Acts. Sadly, much of the preaching in the American church is lukewarm, seeker friendly, and without the manifestation of the Holy Spirit. Faith and the fear of God is absent. People live like there is no tomorrow or eternity.

The church is to represent the kingdom of God on the earth as a living, breathing organism and a replica of the Kingdom of heaven. In heaven there is Love—pure love—no sickness, hatred, anger, fear, and resentment. Only Love. The few brave souls who do seek out the church for solutions, unfortunately find bickering, greed, division, jealousy, and control instead of love displayed.

Many years ago, I was a part of a thriving group of believers in New York City comprised of ex-drug addicts, ex-prostitutes, ex-alcoholics, ex-homosexuals, ex-homeless, ex-witches, ex criminals, etc. Everyone was accepted. Jesus said come as you are and He will deliver you of what ails you. It was a joyful group who eagerly anticipated the weekly meetings to be in the presence of God as their lives were being transformed by the Spirit of God.

Every time we gathered together, the presence of God was tangible and God met the needs of the people. Those of us in leadership made ourselves available to help anyone who needed help by giving time and finances sacrificially. This church was a haven for people from all walks of life who came to be free from sin and get high on the Holy Spirit!

The church is to be a lifeline for those who are drowning in their lives of sin. Unfortunately, most of the American churches are nothing more than social clubs for the elite. It is time to wake up as our redemption is drawing near. In other nations, revival is happening under very difficult circumstances. There is not time for an elite social club or even passivity about one's salvation.

Women warriors, our eyes must be on the things above, not focused on the things of earth. Jesus promised to meet our needs so we should not worry about those things. Instead, we should be focused on our kingdom role in these last days.[39] We should make it a habit in our lives to focus on doing the will of God first. Our minds should be on the kingdom of heaven first. This will help us to get through the difficult times, filled with trials and persecutions. Why focus on laying up treasures on the earth if our riches are in heaven?[40] God does promise to bless us but that should not be our primary focus.[41]

I leave you with this challenge: The harvest is ripe, and the laborers are few! Why are the laborers so few? Most people, like the people in Noah's day, are partying, marrying, and making merry. They have no time to do the will of God as they live only to have a good time. Jesus informed the disciples:

> *"The harvest truly is great, but the laborers are few; therefore pray the Lord of the harvest to send out laborers into His harvest."* (Luke 10:2)

We must redeem the time. God will give us back the lost time the enemy has stolen even in our minds and bodies if we will surrender all to God and let go of our agenda for His agenda. Some are sowers, sowing the seed of the Gospel and others are reaping behind them. So never consider the work you do for God to be inferior. God does not see it that way; only man may look at it in that light. People are seeking other activities to fill their day such as social media.

> *And as it was in the days of Noah, so it will be also in the days of the Son of Man: they ate, they drank, they married wives, they were given in marriage, until the day that Noah entered the ark, and the flood came and destroyed them all. Likewise as it was in the days of Lot: they ate, they drank, they bought, they sold, they planted, they built; but on the day Lot went out of Sodom it rained fire and brimstone from heaven and destroyed*

them all. Even so will it be in the day when the Son of Man is revealed. (Luke 17:26-30)

The church is, indeed, under siege in many countries, including America. Persecution is on the rise everywhere you look, but God sees to it that when the enemy comes in like a flood, God raises up a standard against him. I've seen this in my own life as I ministered in various places. I had to use my sword and shield and stand firm as a courageous warrior with the power of the Holy Spirit. I could not even begin to fight in my own strength. However, once I relinquished the battle to the Lord, He fought for me. I had to first walk by faith and not by sight. I had to expect the impossible and believe to see what I was speaking come to pass.

During these times I learned the power of the spoken word to see God manifest His peace and power and to see the enemy flee. I had to learn not to rely upon my own understanding but to rely upon the Holy Spirit. When we get angry at the devil and make demands on him, God shows up in a big way!

Everyday, we must recall that no weapon formed against us will succeed and every tongue cursing us is condemned by God, our heavenly Father. Yes, sometimes we may get wounded on the battlefield, but the church is to be there for us to heal and bring peace. Unfortunately, and sadly, this is usually not the case. The Holy Spirit is grieved about this lack of caring and power in the American church.

Every day I decree and declare that I am God's battle axe and weapon of war against the enemy to redeem lost souls. We speak for our King Jesus on this earth. The church is in the world but not of the world, but sadly, today is like it was in the days of Lot. People are buying and selling, planting and building towards one goal . . . to become rich.

> *But seek first the kingdom of God and His righteousness, and all these things shall be added to you.* (Matt. 6: 33)

Everyday, as I read the news headlines, it seems America is becoming more and more depraved . . . and divided, even in the church.

> *I saw another angel coming down from heaven, having great authority, and the earth was illuminated with his glory. And He cried mightily with a loud voice, saying, "Babylon the great is fallen, is fallen, and has become a dwelling place of demons, a prison for every foul spirit, and a cage for every unclean and hated bird! For all the nations have drunk of the wine of the wrath of her fornication, the kings of the earth have committed fornications with her, and the merchants of the earth have become rich through the abundance of her luxury." And I heard another voice from heaven saying, "Come out of her, my people, lest you share in her sins, and lest you receive of her plaques. For her sins have reached to heaven, and God has remembered her iniquities. Render to her just as she rendered to you, and repay her double according to her works; in the cup which she has mixed, mix double for her. In the measure that she glorified herself and lived luxuriously, in the same measure give her torment and sorrow; for she says in her heart, "I sit as queen, and am no widow, and will not see sorrow." Therefore her plagues will come in one*

> *day—death and mourning and famine. And she will be utterly burned with fire, for strong is the Lord God who judges her.* (Rev. 18:1-8)

Yes, God has His servants, His laborers, and although they be few, they are reaping great results. They are not focused on politics unless that is their calling from God. The Gospel of Jesus and the Kingdom of God is their banner.

This is our time to go forth in courage as women warriors. God will empower us to do His will!

> *We have this treasure in earthen vessels, that the excellence of the power may be of God and not of us. We are hard-pressed on every side, yet not crushed; we are perplexed, but not in despair; persecuted, but not forsaken; struck down, but not destroyed—always carrying about in the body the dying of the Lord Jesus, that the life of Jesus also may be manifested in our body. For we who live are always delivered to death for Jesus' sake, that the life of Jesus also may be manifested in our body. For we who live are always delivered to death for Jesus' sake, that the life of Jesus also may be manifested in our mortal flesh. So then death is working in us, but life in you.* (2 Cor. 4:7-12)

Lana Vawser saw in her dream women speaking in stadiums all over the world bringing souls to the Lord and being empowered by the Holy Spirit. Yes, it is happening now! People all over the world are looking in all the wrong places for peace and security. It is only found in Jesus, and we have the answer that so few have heard or experienced. God is opening many doors for His women warriors.

Please accept this challenge and answer the call of God to go forth and complete the tasks He has given us to do for His kingdom. To God be all the glory! Yes, and Amen!

> *"How beautiful are the feet of those who preach the gospel of peace, Who bring glad tidings of good things!"* (Rom. 10:15)

Paul speaks of running the race with endurance. That is how we must run, with perseverance to finish well. We must have resilience so that even when we fail, we can get back up and keep going. Failures don't define who you are, as you learn from mistakes and now are better for it.

God will give you the courage to move forward and fulfill the dream He gave you. He has given me the dream to be the voice for the voiceless and to keep fighting to win this war against the darkness.

Women, we can't fear those who desire to ruin our reputations due to jealousy or create conflict and strife around us. When we emerge as leaders, we can become a target for those living unfulfilled lives. We must keep our eyes on Jesus at all times and not on the problems others are creating for us. We acknowledge our battle scars and move on. God has called us to persevere as He fights our battles for us.

We should honor the elderly women such as Anna who stayed in the temple of God, interceding daily waiting to see the Messiah. She must have had the faith that she would one day see the Lamb of God.

We have a great responsibility in the last days to bring revival throughout the world. God has given us the ability to bring in the final harvest!

FINAL PRAYER:

Thank You, Jesus, for the victor's crowns for past, present, and future victories, due to Your blood! May my words glorify You, Jesus. Fine tune my ears, heart, and mind to heaven's frequency. No more siting in the seat of the last season. Thank You for giving us a new seat at the table with all authority and power![42] *I loose warring angels, fire angels, angels of destruction from the throne room, guardian angels, protection angels, ministering angels, and breakthrough angels! You are making me a new sharp threshing instrument with sharp teeth. You are making me Your battle axe and weapon of war.*[43] *You are shining me up, doing a new thing. I'm undaunted, without intimidation, and completely restored. I commune with You, Jesus, for blessings and breakthrough. Thank You, Jesus, for giving me a white stone a NEW name! Amen.*

ADVENTURES IN GOD

"I give my Lord and Savior Jesus Christ all the glory for these amazing victories as I can do nothing without him." ~MK

IMMOBILIZED IN HIS PRESENCE BY THE FIRE OF GOD

One evening I was ministering in the South Pacific Islands at an International Women's meeting. It was a glorious time of worship. I gave the Word of the Lord and then felt led to encourage the women present to expect signs and wonders. God showed up in a big way as His presence permeated the atmosphere. Women were refreshed, healed, delivered, and filled with the Holy Spirit. A couple of us were so overwhelmed by the glory of God we were frozen in place. One woman testified that the fire of God came upon her as she was immobilized in His presence!

CORPORATE HEALING MANIFESTED AT SCHOOL

I had been ministering and teaching at a training center in the Himalayan Mts. for about a week as guest lecturer and noticed that most of the students were suffering from illnesses and/or pains. At the end of the class sessions a few came for prayer, and God healed and delivered them. On the last day, the Lord directed me to have the entire class make a huge circle holding hands and pray for God to touch everyone. He did! A mighty wind came into that room and all the students were slain in the Spirit. When they stood to their feet they were without pain or sickness.

Beauty Shop Deliverance

While living in the Himalayan Mts., one morning my devotional time with the Lord was extended and His presence came in a powerful way. I sensed God desired to use me that day for a special assignment. In the afternoon the Lord directed me to a friend's beauty shop. She had been having some health issues and her blood pressure was suddenly very high. Her doctor desired to hospitalize her. She had shared her concerns with me the week before. As I was on the way to the shop, the Lord reminded me that she had recently begun taking Yoga classes via her television at the shop. As soon as I entered the shop I asked about her health. She expressed that she had not improved. I also asked if she was continuing to take Yoga classes via television. She replied, "Yes." And she was also repeating the chants the teacher was speaking. The Lord revealed to me she had taken in demonic spirits through the Yoga. She repented and consented for me to pray for her. I prayed and commanded the evil spirits to go. They manifested and departed. She was now breathing normally and was instantly healed.

The Lame Walk and the Deaf Mute Sings

I had been ministering at a Himalayan Mt. church and conducting trainings for pastors and leaders. Many people attended these meetings, whether or not they were a pastor or leader. In one of the meetings, during worship, a teenage boy approached me without saying a word. I put my arm around him and began to pray. However, I didn't know what to pray for so I asked the Lord, and He told me to touch his lips with my hand. I did and kept praying for a little while. A few minutes later he cried out in a loud voice like that of a newborn baby. He had been a deaf mute at birth and now could hear and speak. Praise God! Some months later when I returned to that church, he was learning to sing songs!

At that same church a crippled man was instantly healed and began to dance around the church, proclaiming in English (although he didn't know much English) what God Almighty had done for him as the Holy Spirit fell upon him.

God Holds the Mountains in His Hands

In the spring of 2015, the Himalayan Mts. had a 7.9 and an 8.0 earthquake and many aftershocks for months. People were stranded in the high mountains without food or clean water. The military helicopters could not reach many smaller villages them to drop food supplies due to thick dense forests and inability to see the villages.

After much prayer, my team and I decided to deliver food and water to the villagers stranded on the mountain top. The newspapers reported that aftershocks made this trip too dangerous. We prayed for God's protection and safe passage to the top and back down without any incidents.

My assistant and her father, a pastor, and my cinematographer left early one morning for the village of Asenec, where the pastor's mother and brother lived on the summit. The trip took three hours on a motorcycle before the earthquake; however, today the roads were washed out and the clay made the roads slippery Even large trucks were stuck on the road. The old truck we were traveling in was straining every inch of the way. Eight hours later we arrived at the top of the mountain and distributed the goods to the people. The pastor's sister-in-law had died in the earthquake and his mother suffered a compound fracture of her leg.

During the next several months, as we made trips back to that village, we prayed for God to transport us and keep the mountains at peace. The Lord answered our prayers, and the last trip took only three and a half hours to reach the summit.

Instant Healing of Heart and Lungs

As my assistant and I entered a Himalayan Mountain church, a man entered behind us carrying a woman. He dropped her on a long bench in the back of the church, laying her flat on her back. It was obvious she was having difficulty breathing. He looked at us as we inquired about her condition. He replied, "You pray for her, and Jesus will heal her!" He added, "It's a heart condition."

The worship service began in about ten minutes and as the presence of God filled the sanctuary, the Lord prompted me to walk to the back of the church with my anointing oil, lean over her, and begin to pray. Soon she struggled to sit up. I asked her if she could stand up. She nodded her head in the affirmative. She stood up and took a few steps as I led her outside to breathe in fresh air. She gained strength in her body and took in the fresh air. She was healed by the power of God! Her mother and sisters were filled with joy, thanking and praising God.

Touching Heaven, Changing Earth

Once or twice a year I organized times of worship for Himalayan Mt. youth to come together from many area churches. I met with a nucleus of youth leaders representing their various churches for event planning. We rotated the host church every time we gathered for the event. We began worshipping about 11a.m. and would continue until 5 - 6 p.m. with a fifteen-minute tea break after a few hours. The youth were thrilled to invite the presence of God with singing and dancing. Worship leaders from different churches took turns leading the worship. This was a time to glorify the Lord Jesus Christ.

At the beginning of the program, a young lady approached me informing me she had been diagnosed with a brain tumor, and she was very worried as the doctors were recommending surgery. I expressed this was a time to focus on Jesus, worshipping Him, and He will come and heal her. I said not to focus on her situation but to pray and worship the Lord. She closed her eyes and began worshipping the Lord Jesus Christ. The power and presence of God filled the place and people were being healed of emotional wounds.

Several weeks later the same young lady called to meet with me and said she had great news! God had healed her—the symptoms and the tumor disappeared. Doctors confirmed the healing by an MRI that was taken following the youth worship program.

HINDU PRIEST HEALED AND DELIVERED

One day a Hindu priest in the Himalayan Mts. approached one of my pastor friends seeking help for illnesses that he and his wife were suffering. He stated healings came for others who paid him money but not for him and his wife. The pastor explained to him about Jesus Christ, the Savior, Healer, and Deliverer. The man and his family agreed to give their lives to Jesus, repented of their sins, and were healed.

He had a long fight ahead against the evil powers of darkness, but he persevered and in about a year he was completely free of tormenting spirits. This man and his family were an inspiration to me during a difficult time I was experiencing. They remained faithful and consistent in serving Jesus Christ no matter what was happening to them. He gave up his livelihood as a priest and began farming. God blessed him to be successful in agriculture. Not a Sabbath day went by that he didn't give God 10 percent of his profits. He was very faithful in this area although he had little funds. Every time I met them, they were smiling and praising God.

The Church That Was Built in a Day

I was invited by a pastor that I was not acquainted with to speak in his Himalayan Mt. church. A mutual pastor friend had recommended me to him. He informed me that his church was small, only fifteen people. I agreed to go there and upon arrival found th situation less than ideal. The pastor asked me not to mention the Holy Spirit when I spoke. I found his wife in deep depression. They had been married a few years and were barren, without children, which in that culture is a disgrace.

As we began to worship, three teenage boys in the row in front of me began shaking and trembling every time I raised my hands to praise God. After the worship I preached a salvation message on the love of God. People continued entering the church until there were maybe seventy or eighty people. It was a storefront church. Some were probably coming out of curiosity.

When I gave the invitation to receive Jesus, many women and children came forward praying earnestly for their sins to be forgiven. The presence of the Holy Spirit came, and tears flowed freely among them as they welcomed His presence. I realized that without the infilling of the Holy Spirit, they would have difficulties and spiritual conflicts upon returning to their homes—i.e. spiritual warfare. I asked the pastor if I could preach another message on the Holy Spirit. He said, "Yes, but only for ten minutes."

As I preached about the Holy Spirit; the women and children came to the front, opening up their hearts. The Holy Spirit came like a mighty rushing wind and the teenage boys were soon on the floor slithering like snakes. The Holy Spirit instructed me to ignore them as they were possessed by evil spirits and the Holy Spirit would deliver them. I continued to go through the crowd praying for people to receive the Holy Spirit, and even the men responded. The pastor was focused on his wife who had been slain in the spirit and was laughing out loud as the Holy Spirit flooded her being.

When the service finished about an hour later (so much for the ten minutes) all were rejoicing, and the teenage boys were completely free. Standing up, they looked like new people. Many were saved, healed, and delivered that day, including the pastor who had been mixing Jesus with Buddhism. The pastor called our mutual friend the next day and excitedly stated the church was built in a day! He said the wife was laying hands on people and seeing them healed and filled with the Holy Spirit. Less than a year later she conceived, and they had a beautiful baby boy! The teenagers were now youth leaders, seeing other teens delivered and filled with the Holy Spirit. A few years later I visited them again, and they had close to 200 attendees and a new building. Only GOD could do a miracle and build a church in one day!

[1] Est. 5:1-3

2 Smith, William, *Dr. Smith's Bible Dictionary*, "Entry for Sceptre," 1901, quoted *Wikipedia*, https://en.wikipedia.org>wiki>Sceptre.

[3] MK Henderson, Healing and Restoring Children at Risk: A Practical Guide for Caregivers of Traumatized Children, 2nd ed. (KDP, 2019), 29.

[4] Henderson, *Healing and Restoring Children at Risk,* 31.

[5] Est. 2:7-9

[6] John 4:7-26

[7] Matt. 28:1-10

[8] Prov. 23:7

[9] https://hermeneutics.stackexchange.com/questions/5767/why-does-moses-change-hoseas-name-to-joshua

[10] Isa. 22:22-23

[11] Jer. 29:11

[12] Dr. Marina McLean, Appetite for Worship: Creating a Hunger for His Presence (Bedford, TX: Creative Enterprises Studio, 2017), 45.

[13] Ps. 110:3

[14] Heb. 7:11

[15] Kevin Basconi, *Unlocking the Hidden Mysteries of the Seer Anointing* (King of Glory Ministries International, 2015), 35.

[16] Basconi, *Unlocking Mysteries,* 37.

[17] Heb. 7:1-2

[18] Barbie Beathitt, Dream Encounters: Seeing Your Destiny from God's Perspective (Barbie Breathitt Enterprises, 2009), 134-135.

[19] Rom. 16:20

[20] 1 John 3:8

[21] Beathitt, Dream Encounters, 134.

[22] Ps. 91:1-4

[23] Beathitt, *Dream Encounters,* 135. (1 Cor. 2:9)

[24] Beathitt, *Dream Encounters,* 138-139. (Heb. 11:3)

[25] Beathitt, *Dream Encounters,* 143-145. (Prov. 24:16)

[26] Prov. 4:18

[27] 1 John 4:18

[28] 2 Cor. 4:18

[29] Ps. 91

[30] Chuck Pierce on gloryofzion.org/prophecy center etc.

[31] Est. 1-6

[32] Col. 2:10

[33] Daniel and Amber Pierce, *Joy in the War* (Charisma House, 2022), 37.

[34] Pierce, *Joy in the War,* 90.

[35] Pierce, *Joy in the War,* 164.

[36] Becca Greenwood, *Authority to Tread* (Destiny Image, year), 21.

[37] Ps. 144:1

[38] R. Arthur Matthews, *Ready for Battle Studies in Christian Discipleship,* (Wheaton, IL: Harold Shaw, 1993),123.

[39] Matt. 6:33

[40] Luke 12:20

[41] Deut. 8:18

[42] Hag. 2:2

[43] Jer. 51:20

www.ingramcontent.com/pod-product-compliance
Lightning Source LLC
Chambersburg PA
CBHW070452100426
42743CB00010B/1588